TWO OR THREE TOGETHER

HARPER'S MINISTERS PAPERBACK LIBRARY

Two or Three Together

A Manual for Prayer Groups

BY

HAROLD WILEY FREER

AND

FRANCIS B. HALL

HARPER & ROW, PUBLISHERS
New York, Hagerstown, San Francisco, London

TWO OR THREE TOGETHER

Copyright, 1954, by Harper & Row, Publishers, Inc.

Printed in the United States of America

First Harper & Row paperback edition published in 1977.

ISBN: 0-06-063031-0

Library of Congress catalogue card number: 54-5849

77 78 79 80 81 10 9 8 7 6 5 4 3 2 1

DEDICATION

To the members of the prayer groups with which we have had most intimate relationships, those in Dover Congregational Church, Westlake, Ohio, and those in New York City and Kingwood Community whose willingness to experiment reverently in prayer and the devotional life helped create this book

Preface

Growth in the spiritual life requires a group. Within one's own spirit one must make those lonely decisions out of which the desire to grow arises, but this desire needs the nurture of fellowship with others as well as with God. True enough, God may be found on the golf course or in the woods or mountains, both on Sundays and on weekdays. But those spots, valuable though they may be, are not the growing ground for one's spiritual life.

In fellowship with other like-minded folk, earnestly seeking to know and understand the will of God, comes the practice of the presence of God. Their counsel, their experience, their questionings, their faith are the nourishment we need, the encouragement to keep on, the joy that delights us in knowing that we do not stand alone in our search. These too, our friends, with us have turned their faces toward the Light.

Sometimes within the Church itself, or under its sponsorship, yet many times beyond the pale of the Church, these groups come together. Here is the mood of worship, where adoration, confession, petition, intercession, offering may take place. Weekly meeting together in silence and meditation and sharing gives one the ground for his daily living, which inevitably, regardless of the crowd around, must be lived alone. But without that group worship, without that sense of fellowship with others, one fights a losing battle.

So these suggestions that follow, though they may be used by the individual, and will be helpful to him even though he cannot be a member of a group, are guides for the creating of prayer or fellowship groups. They have come out of many years of experimenting with prayer and the devotional life in groups in which both men and women, as well as some young people, have joined.

Although much has already appeared in print regarding the value of prayer groups and the dominant principles of their life, most of it has been in the form of pamphlets, articles and chapters in books. For the most part each of these discussions has been limited to a concern with one of the various possible forms of prayer groups and none of them have offered detailed suggestions regarding the possible content of the sharing, discussion and study of the groups. It is in the hope that these needs may be met that the present book has been prepared.

Part One is a general introduction to prayer groups, what they are, how they function, detailed descriptions of the various kinds. Part Two attempts to answer the question: after a group comes together in chapel or home or office, what do its members talk about, discuss, pray over? It is, if you will, a suggested "curriculum," covering a period of thirty weeks and showing what several prayer groups in one church have worked out during their experimenting together. Part Three is an annotated bibliography of books of many kinds, old and modern classics, that may be of help to prayer groups in their devotional life, in their practice of prayer and in their understanding of the spiritual life.

Not only has the material in this book come into being because of many group experiences but the writing of it has also been a group project. The authorship of Part One is as equally the work of Pearl Hall and Hazel Brownson as of the nominal authors and so full credit is given them. It is the prayer of this small group that the fruit of their corporate work may be of help to other seeking groups out of which may come a new spiritual power sufficient to the needs of our day.

HAROLD WILEY FREER
Westlake, Ohio
FRANCIS B. HALL
Kingwood Community
Frenchtown, N. J.

Contents

9

PART TWO

MEDITATIONS AND HELPS

PART ONE

The Life of Prayer Groups

I

Why Prayer Groups?

What is our most imperative need? It is the need for relatedness—the need to love. We are lonely for ourselves, for our neighbors and for our God. Our unhappy behavior roots in our inability to love. By love we mean a capacity for the experience of concern, responsibility, respect and understanding of other persons, as well as an intense desire for the growth of other persons. That we must be brethren is the fundamental law of our being.

After a half century of probing into the minds of modern men and women, psychiatrists are reiterating that the prime need of every person is to be loved and to be loving. Relatedness, they say, is the panacea for our predominating neurosis—isolation of spirit. We are driven to find the methods and formulas that will transform basic loneliness into basic loveliness, that will revolutionize negativity into creativity.

The character of society has been changed again and again throughout history when human beings have experienced a desperate need. When they have no longer been able to depend on surface satisfactions, they have explored physical and spiritual resources for the renewing of life. Hunger and thirst have ever served to push the human family into such adventures of body and spirit that a new level of life has been discovered. Since this has been the experience of the past, we can with courage and hope face the demands of our own age.

When a drought threatens the willow tree new vitality stirs in its roots—they creep around and over the most formidable obstacles to reach life-giving water—even penetrating the sealed joints of sewer pipes. So it is with us human beings. Our sure instinct—our inherent sense that life is worth while only because we belong to

15

one another and to God—impels us to penetrate whatever barriers our mechanical society has erected. Unless the root of our basic unity is activated we will remain frustrated, stunted individuals.

The fundamental need of the race for togetherness is being manifested in a spontaneous upsurge of small groups in every area—secular and religious. Small companies are the order of the day. Labor-management is experimenting with various techniques for establishing interpersonal connections between workers. GI's are allowed to train, live and fight in four-man teams. Belonging to one another multiplies each man's courage, the militarists say. Psychotherapists are accomplishing astonishing recoveries with neurotics through small-group activities. WANA—We Are Not Alone—is the name of one such group that has reduced the number of mental hospital returns from 80 to 33 per cent.

But relatedness to one another alone is not the panacea. The quest for salvation from war, revolution, terrifying dictatorships, atomic and bacteriological menaces, as well as the quest for integration of deteriorating psyches, have sent us along many strange and, in the end, futile paths. The thirsty root of the tree tangling with the obstacles on its own level does not entirely sustain the graceful tree above ground. The earthward thrust combined with the skyward stretch changes the character of the tree. It is the upward reach that makes the prayer group more effective than any other kind of small group. The members of the spiritual life group aspire to relatedness with God both as individuals and as a unit of the Kingdom of God.

A strong hope of the human family finding its true connection with the purposes of God lies in just such little companies. One stronghold after another of our man-made fortresses has failed us. Philosophers, psychologists, sociologists, theologians and even scientists are not so cocksure today as many of them were once that the destiny of man lies in political and social systems. It is becoming more and more evident that those who have waited on the Lord, patiently reaching for the high free sky of His Presence, have fed the basic hunger of the human family.

This book is concerned with this double relatedness of men. Salvation lies in its establishment. If we believe this we must assume that there is a power more than human that rests in the heart at the innermost core of every man, and that at the same time pervades the whole universe, not only pervading it but giving it being, life and meaning. We must further assume that this power can come into the world through the lives of men and women who seek it and open themselves to it. The seeking and opening have always been more easily done when people band themselves together to give mutual assistance in the seeking. "Where two or three are gathered together in my name, there am I in the midst" is verified over and over again. A community of life and guidance from the Presence—the Holy Spirit—emerges so that a purer ethic and a more eager confidence in sustaining it than ever existed before can develop.

Prayer groups that have thus transformed the character of the human family have been for the most part anonymous. They have been as the leaven in the meal, the seed buried in the earth, the pearl lost in the field. William James sensed their potency in this way: "I am *against* bigness and greatness in all their forms and *with* the invisible, molecular moral forces that work from individual to individual, stealing in through the crannies of the world, like so many soft rootlets or like the capillary oozing of water, and yet rending the hardest monuments of man's pride, if you give them time."

THE WITNESS OF HISTORY

The rise of Christianity itself exemplifies the breaking through of the Holy Spirit into the consciousness of a gathered and expectant group. Although through the centuries the Jews had been enslaved, threatened by wars and annihilation, demoralized by false idols, yet they were preserved by the expectation of a Messiah, promised over and over again by their prophets who imperiously called them back to the worship of the one true God and to obedience to His law. Thus it happened that men who were dedicated to listening to the Divine whisper proved to be the salvation of Israel. Expectant waiting reached its peak in the first century before Christ. Among small communities of the period were the Essenes. This group developed a devout and disciplined openness to God. John the Baptist was an indirect, if not a direct, disciple of their resolute teachings, and Jesus himself possibly had more than a casual contact with them.

Small groups of earnest people with religious concern inevitably gathered together about any person who gave promise of being a prophet of God. That stout-hearted men should attach themselves to Jesus was therefore to be expected. The discovery that Jesus himself was the Son of God was a wonder far surpassing their deepest longing. Even though their expectation was dimmed out by the crucifixion, it lived again in the resurrection. The risen Christ put in their hands the key that would release the waiting Spirit of God and let it flow through them into the wastes of the world. They were commissioned to "watch and pray" *together* until the Holy Spirit came.

All together in one place they waited, prayed and worshiped. Into their midst swept the Pentecostal Spirit. It poured on them and through them like a mighty torrent bursting through a dam. It rushed out into the world, sweeping up thousands and carrying them along; it divided and subdivided and spread until it penetrated the farthermost corners of the earth. It was a magic stream, for although it flowed far from its fountainhead in Jerusalem, its power was always potentially as great as at the beginning. Although it flowed onto deserts and was soaked up in thirsty sand, or ran against barriers and became stagnant and foul, the original power was always there *in potentia*. Thus time and again at crucial points in history it has burst forth in stalwart souls and small groups devoted to the search for Truth and Love with such dynamic energy that it has transformed society, turning men again and again toward their true and eternal goal.

Compromise with Constantine marked a trend toward worldly materialism in the Church. Massiveness became greatness with many of the church leaders. Political power, numerical strength, economic security became valid ends for which the virtue of relatedness to God and man might be lawfully sacrificed. To the degree that the Church substituted military valor for spiritual courage it lost "the greatest force in the world"—the Holy Spirit of God's love. In the tragic era that ensued, civilization sank deeper into despairing darkness, yet the glow did not fade out altogether. Small communities of men and women, bound together by their common search for the Lord, sprang up like flickering candles bringing hope to the human family threatened with chaotic gloom. These Benedictine communities preserved the treasures of civilization, rejuvenated agriculture, and led the way to a rebirth of society.

Although we might discover in the sources of the Franciscan orders and the beginnings of the Protestant Reformation similar groups of sincere searchers—such as the early Hutterian Brothers who were obviously related to the social disorder of the time—we will turn directly to those bands of seekers that later gave rise to Quakerism and then to Methodism.

The seventeenth and eighteenth centuries in England were marked by turmoil, revolution and counterrevolution, oppression and unrest. The Reformation, long delayed in England, was played out and did not produce a virile church as it had on the Continent. The life of religion was suppressed by form and dogma, ecclesiastical strife and persecution. Hearts of spiritually sensitive men and women were hungry and thirsty. In order to find a way to satisfy their souls, these individuals began to seek out one another and to meet together in homes to pray and zealously to explore the Scriptures. It was not an organized movement so much as a spontaneous impulse to seek together for a firsthand experience of the Divine. This tendency manifested itself throughout the whole nation—from Wales to the far places of Scotland. Various names were given to these unorthodox bands, but the name most commonly used was The Seekers.

George Fox is typical of many young men of his time who were determined to find the primal peace of soul that results from the coming of the Holy Spirit. "Into his soul's distress," he wrote later, "there came the Word of God saying that there was one, Christ Jesus, who could speak to his condition." The discovery of the living Spirit launched Fox on a mission that found an immediate response among the groups of Seekers which later united to form "The Children of Light"—or the early Religious Society of Friends. Mere mention is made here of the reforming energy that moved through these early Quakers: in the struggle for religious liberty, in the reform of penal and mental institutions, in the freeing of slaves, in reconciliation of warring nations, their power for good manifested itself.

After the rise of the Quakers, unrest in England continued into the next century, moving toward revolutionary tension. Seeking groups continued to be formed. Young John Wesley belonged to one such fellowship of prayer during his stay at Oxford. Later, after a tempestuous ministry in America where he came into contact with earnest communities of followers of Zinzendorf, he returned to England. He was burdened with the futility of his own efforts to heal the distress, poverty and violence that circled him; he was lonely and rejected by his mother church. In the depths of his despair he went one evening to a small meeting of poor Dissenters at Aldersgate, where men and women were keeping the fire of their hearts aglow by prayer and love. It seemed to him that the very heats of heaven warmed his heart that evening. So inflamed was he by the power of the Spirit that he carried the torch up and down the roads of England, setting other hearts aglow. He bound his converts into little class meetings where the outcast and wretched found companionship, and through these simple gatherings there was released a Spirit that transformed the lives of working men and women everywhere. It is said by some historians that this spiritual awakening prevented a violent revolution in England and paved the way for the ascendancy of a truly democratic society.

The Current Scene

Can another spiritual awakening with its power to overcome fear and hate and reduce the barriers between men come into the world? Can men once again know that love which will lift them out of themselves into a new sense of oneness with all creation? If history means anything, the answer is Yes! The prerequisite for an awakening, as we have indicated already, is a desire for seeking, a hunger for the Divine. If we wait on the Lord, if we call upon Him, if we seek Him with all our hearts, we are ever sure to find Him. Relatedness is established. The more widespread that seeking is, the most significant will be the finding. The most sanguine hope of the times, then, is this extraordinary and spontaneous drawing together of men and women into small groups—both in and out of the churches—to seek the Source of life and love.

The present prayer group movement began about twenty years ago as a spontaneous activity in all parts of Christendom. There have never been any central headquarters nor organizing secretaries to sponsor the upsurge of prayer units now taking place. Men and women are coming together naturally for mutual help in tapping the springs of spiritual strength simply because they have a need. It is a genuine grass roots affair: the natural reaction, it would seem, of lonely people caught in an age of crisis and of fear.

After World War I the college campus became a center of deep spiritual searching on the part of students whose integrity would not permit them to accept blindly the traditional dogmas of the Church, and yet whose faith held them back from a humanistic agnosticism. Those same students are the men and women who today are influencing the spiritual exploration now going on in the religious scene.

In 1941 the Malvern Conference issued a challenge to the Church indicating that the time was ripe for the establishment of a disciplined *Third Order* among the congregations. The need for communities of "athletes of the spirit" was deeply impressed upon the Conference. In 1948 the movement received a second impetus. After the World Christian Conference in Oslo a group of students committed themselves to the nurture of fellowship among all student prayer groups of the world. Out of this concern came The Life Stream Foundation, with a house for student living and meetings adjacent to the campus of the University of California. A small magazine is published regularly by the Foundation to carry news of prayer group activities to the four corners of the earth.

Another seed bed for prayer groups has been Calvary Church in New York City. A large part of the scanty bibliography available on prayer groups is supplied by pamphlets and leaflets that have developed out of the experience of prayer groups meeting in this church.

On a wider scale of influence are the Laymen's Movement for a Christian World and the Camps Farthest Out. Both groups have unquestioning faith in the power of prayer to affect the political course of history and have led in the stimulating and setting up of groups committed to finding and using Divine power in bringing peace.

As "an alternative to futility" various church organizations on a national scale are encouraging the growth of spiritual fellowships by means of their women's organizations, boards of evangelism, spiritual life committees. There is no way of telling how many groups there are in this country to say nothing of the world. For all those that come into being through the stimulation of an organization there are probably many more that have been formed because of an individual who had himself shared in a group experience or been inspired by the writings of such men as Douglas Steere, Elton Trueblood, Allan Hunter, Roy Burkhart, Samuel Shoemaker, Glenn Clark, Harvey Seifert, Gerald Heard.

As seekers were many in England at the time of George Fox and John Wesley, so they abound today. A bird's-eye view of present little gatherings is not very different from that of two or three centuries ago.

Small groups of men and women gathered in town and country homes and sat together in silence to "wait on the Lord." In their countenances and bearing there was awe and reverence, as if they were gathered, not in a simple living room, but in a holy temple. Expectancy pervaded the group like that felt by those who wait the coming of a great person or the occurrence of an important event, yet it was obvious from the expression of their faces that attention was directed not without but within. Some heads were bowed in wordless prayer, others uplifted as if gazing at supernal light. At times, unpredictably, the silence was broken by a voice pleading for submission to the divine Will or by words of supplication to God.[1]

In the next chapters we shall examine the various manifestations and workings of such groups—groups that can be so instrumental in the transformation of men and society. We shall learn from the experiences of various fellowships of prayer ways in which we may tap divine Sources and Resources for the power to love with all our mind and will and strength.

[1] Howard Brinton: *Friends for 300 Years* (New York: Harper & Brothers, 1952), p. 1.

II

What Is the Nature of Prayer Groups?

WHAT IS A PRAYER GROUP?

Quick answers might be: "a fellowship of athletes of the spirit"; "a vigorous community of seekers"; "a working team like Peter, James and John among the disciples." In fact, the prayer group is a small, intimate comradeship, united in a common commitment which through regular group discipline seeks spiritual power and direction. The disciples well illustrate such a group. Their chief concern was to be near Jesus, to learn from him, to work with him and to pray with him.

What shall we call a group of this kind? Thus far we have been designating it by the term prayer group. Other names are "fellowship group," "fellowship of the concerned." A term common among many religious seekers is "the cell." Although this word has a political association for some people it so fittingly describes the work and purpose of the prayer group that we shall use it interchangeably in the following chapters. A cell is a unit of life, a means to growth, and joins with other life for a specific purpose.

Still another term is "atom," for like the atom, a company engaged in prayer can create a field of force greater than the sum of its parts. "A man, be the heavens ever praised, is sufficient for himself, yet were ten men, united in love, capable of being and doing what ten thousand singly would fail in." [1]

Today we know that the atom is a complex structure, held together by various forces within itself and composed of a nucleus, itself complex, and a number of whirling electrons. Packed into every atom is an appalling power that can be released under the

[1] Thomas Carlyle, quoted in A Group of Ten, Lane Hall leaflet.

right conditions. The prayer group has its component parts, its nucleus of faithful members, and locked within it is tremendous power that under the proper conditions may be released, either as a catalytic agent—the leaven of the Spirit—or as an amazing explosion of spiritual power as at Pentecost. Dr. Leslie Weatherhead has stated that one such active group in a church can in time vitalize or revitalize the whole congregation. The power is there to be released, but the conditions for the releasing must be just right.

The first right condition that transforms a collection of persons into an atom with power-potential is fellowship. The group does not catch fire unless all its members have a keen sense of belonging. All the members unconsciously say "we" instead of "they" or "you" when referring to the affairs of the group. All must have a relationship of concern for one another.

The second right condition is mutual strengthening. As Muriel Lester puts it: "It is through the fellowship of the Catacombs that the early Christians achieved the courage of the Coliseum." So the ancient Hasidim had an expression: "When one man would sing and cannot lift his voice, there comes one who can lift his voice and together they make glorious music."

A third right condition to make a group dynamic is mutual enlightening. A shared wisdom opens the minds and hearts so that each has a new light on the meaning of life, on the nature of man, and on the guidance for the path that he is to follow. In a sincere group of seekers the light shines through all the windows, so to speak, instead of through one big picture window—and each affords a different view. No window is too small to let the radiance of God through.

The fourth right condition necessary is corporate inspiration. One soul afire kindles another. "We took sweet counsel together," said the Psalmist, "and walked into the house of God in company."

A story is told of an intercessory prayer cell in a large city, made up of hardworking women who found themselves often too tired to welcome the thought of another meeting. Each time before one woman went she would say to her husband, "I just can't go out again tonight," but she always went; and every time she would come home all aglow with the joy of the glorious fellowship that she had experienced. It was one of this group, a harried little laundress, who said, "Here inside of me I have a quiet no man can take from me." The group lighted one another; they prayed for irate cooks as well as for Stalin with an equal fervor and good will. Love and joy and peace are a contagion. The Holy Spirit stirs in the heart of a member and one by one each is kindled to release healing energies into the world.

Akin to this mutual inspiration is the spiritual breakthrough. If members are loyal to their purpose to grow in the love of God and man, they are transformed. Conduct, character, and finally, consciousness, are shaped by the work of the Spirit.

Of course, it is dangerous to look over one's shoulder to see what is happening. Our part is simply to have faith in God. It is even more undesirable to become spiritual end-getters. In loving God with all one's heart, soul, mind and strength, means and ends become one; for ends achieved are in reality but signposts pointing to even greater heights beyond.

We can rejoice in the miracles that happen along the way but we dare not put up a house at any signpost. The disciples had learned from childhood of Elijah and Moses. As they grew in spirit, the meaning and wisdom of these great saintly leaders became incorporated into their own lives. Then came the day when the disciples saw them on the Mount of Transfiguration. But Jesus did not let his disciples stay on the Mount. He pushed them on to the epileptic, to where men were suffering.

Miracles do happen in prayer groups but we must go on from there. "God is alive!" as one young woman put it. "For thirty-five years I have been connected with churches, going to Sunday school and morning worship regularly. I always thought I was a Christian. But reading the Bible and praying were uninteresting chores to me. I did neither if I could help it. But now I cannot do enough reading of the Bible, and I want to thank God all the time. Church is no longer a duty but a joy. And God is alive!" She paused for a moment, then added with surprise, "Could it be that I have been converted?"

Miracles of physical and psychological healing can be described by many. A group made of four couples in a northern state was able to restore one of its members to mental health because of the sustaining love and unfailing patience of the others. Gentleness and understanding with Divine undergirding can produce amazing results as they are put to work by those who "care" for one another.

Fellowships of the concerned inevitably have miracles in their midst. A person who has had years of healing experience says that two requirements are essential: first, faith that opens the door to God's power and peace; second, a caring love that opens the door of the suffering brother or sister to receive this peace. These bring about the miracles of healing, body, mind and soul.

A Prayer Group Must Be Small and Intimate

Only in the small group is it possible on the basis of weekly meetings for each member to come to know the others deeply. Intimate knowledge is essential before there is an unfaltering trust in another. A cell cannot come alive when its members mistrust each other. Then they will protect themselves by playing roles. At best it is not easy for people to leap over the hurdles of their inhibitions and share the faint glimmerings of faith and hope. They must come to know one another as fellow seekers, each with human strengths and weaknesses.

A group of young people spent six weeks together in a social action workshop. They went through several levels of relationship. After four weeks one boy described it thus: "The first week we were all on good behavior and liked one another fairly well. The second week we couldn't keep it up and were our worst selves, so that everyone was disappointed with everyone else, and felt let down by the bunch of phonies that he had for fellow workers. The third week we all came to our senses and decided to make the most of one another and now we know where we stand and are ready to grow."

George Fox thought that six was the ideal number for a missionary team. The Holy Club at Oxford, out of which John Wesley came, numbered the same. Two are enough to begin a cell, twelve is optimum, and fifteen in steady attendance means that it is time to divide the cell.

Many intercessory prayer groups have from twenty-five to seventy-five members. Although they are prayer groups, they cannot achieve the deep fellowship that qualifies them as spiritual atoms. They are different expressions of corporate prayer and worship, as is the church. Each has a valuable work to do and each is a part of the organic whole. But in the cell the emphasis is on cohesiveness as against fragmentation and on developing a unique inner discipline of high quality of which we shall speak in the next chapter.

The Prayer Group Is Bound by a Common Concern

Cohesion results from a variety of forces but none binds members so firmly as devotion to a common goal. No group can live and thrive if its impetus is from without. No group in truth comes into existence unless there is need for it. The need may be particularized—to share, to study, to work out an ideal into practical living form, to meditate together, to make intercession—but beyond any of these needs is an overarching general loyalty to God. Love and faith in Him demand top priority in the scale of values. This common loyalty to the goal to grow in the love of God and man is called by varying terms: to grow spiritually; to become a healing channel of the Holy Spirit; to learn how to "pray unceasingly"; to practice the presence of God.

To implement these concerns the group engages in several forms of activities, no one of which can be absent if the cell is to fulfill its functions. The members seek to grow spiritually by prayer, they share life's experiences, they practice intercessory prayer, and they work and study together specifically for God's glory and the love of their fellow men. It happens most frequently that one of these activities is central, and hence the prayer cell may be called a meditation group, a sharing group, an intercessory group, a workout group or a study group. It also happens that in the course of a cell's life the emphasis may change and an intercessory group may find that it needs to renew its spirit by study or meditation primarily, and one of these activities takes precedence. This change of emphasis will be discussed more fully in succeeding chapters as well as the nature of each of these activities.

1. Prayer and meditation in prayer groups are most generally

informal with a longer period of worship at the beginning of the meeting and a shorter one at the close. These periods of worship are used in a variety of ways but there is a growing practice of silence among all religious groups and this is particularly true of prayer groups.

The purpose of silence is apparent. It is waiting on the Lord. In the Book of Wisdom we have these words, "As all things stood in the midst of silence, and the night had reached the middle of its course, then, O Lord, thy almighty word left its throne and came down to us."

A growing reliance upon silence is in evidence as we study various types of fellowship prayer groups. The silence may have several kinds of settings, but it still is waiting receptively in the Lord's Presence.

First, there is the unbroken, unprogrammed silence for a stated period; second, there is the Quaker form in which various Friends speak as they are led by the Spirit; third, there is the partially programmed silence in which one of the members reads from the Scriptures or a devotional classic, followed by a led meditation or a meditation based on the corporate reading of a prepared paper as described in Part Two of this book.

2. The second activity, sharing, on a personal basis, seems to be negligible in many groups, yet it inevitably happens that as a group reaches maturity there is a spontaneous interchange between the members. No one can go deep into his Divine relationship without finding his interaction with his fellows reaching down also. "A sound man's heart," said an ancient Chinese sage, "is not shut within itself but is open to other peoples' hearts." This is what makes possible group therapy: the give and take of question and comment; the seeking and giving of help; the personal revelation of one's own inner life or the far more joyous insight into God's purposes; the frank pooling of weaknesses and strengths.

3. A third activity is intercession. If this is the purpose of the cell's existence, the renewal of the spirit by prayer for personal purity cannot be omitted, for intercession implies being a channel of God's healing love and joy and peace to others. Whatever the

practice of a group may be, its very concern for one another's growth leads to intercession.

Intercession is a mighty stimulus to spiritual growth as the following letter shows. The woman who wrote it had been called away from home by her sister's death and was kept away by the severe illness of her mother. These two circumstances had laid a heavy burden upon her.

I do appreciate your prayer [she wrote to her cell group]. Last night I was tempted to go to bed without a real prayer period. I had been with mother all evening and had been missing some sleep, so was dead tired. I went out to close the garage door, and the stars were so bright they fairly made me draw in my breath. . . . I stood and looked and looked. When I went back in, I knew I had to take time for meditation. Seating myself in the living room, I took up Oxenham's little booklet, *The Sacraments,* and read those that seemed to speak to my condition and then had a very meaningful period of prayer. This morning as I did the dishes I was thinking how I was, as it were, *drawn* to it, almost beyond my will. Then into my mind there flashed the thought, "Why, it was Thursday night." I think that was my first experience of being moved into action by the power of others' prayers. I've heard people tell of such experiences (as when in concentration camps) but I had never had it happen to me, so far as I know. My thanks to you all. Now I *know* that where "two or three are gathered together . . ." is a promise for today.

4. In the workout group various elements may predominate, but a common project of some sort in any cell cannot be healthily omitted. Jesus' disciples were diligent about keeping themselves in His Presence, but He continually had some work for them to do together—feeding the multitudes, catching fish for breakfast, preaching the gospel. The cell meeting is the place of departure as well as the place for filling up. It is an end in itself but also a means to something further. If cells are to become the healing tissue of the Church, the members will constantly take on more and more responsibility in its affairs. The way of spiritualizing the concerns of life is through groups of devoted Christians who, having prayed and learned together among themselves, are giving themselves to working together. A spiritual atom, no matter what its emphasis,

is no monastery. It is a means to developing a vital Third Order. The famed Third Order of St. Francis was made up of men and women who not only sought to penetrate the innermost parts of their being with the love of Christ but were also seeking to penetrate into the world with that same joyous, enthusiastic love. They trained to make themselves instruments of peace among men. This Third Order became a nursery for saints that in turn transformed the atmosphere of Europe.

5. A fifth activity is study. "Study to show thyself . . . a workman that needeth not to be ashamed." For most groups seeking spiritual development there is a vast ignorance about ways of prayer. An obvious proof of this may be seen in the avidity with which modern and ancient books on the subject are being produced and purchased. Meditation groups may read devotional classics during meals or as a preliminary to meditation. Intercessory and sharing groups turn often to the Bible.

A group of "good" church women had heard a great deal about prayer, but when an urgent need arose for intercession, they faced an inadequacy. Because of this experience they met together to deepen their own faith by worship and study. They were alive and earnest about it. Then Prayer Books became dog-eared, they went afield into other liturgical material, they read the Scriptures and did homework on a series of questions. In time they began a study of the classic forms of prayer. While these active studies were going on, they began, somewhat gingerly at first, to pray. As a result this group, that might be called "a school of prayer," became the mother group of sixty such prayer atoms.

In this chapter we have a mural-like view of prayer groups. Murals are always stimulating, but the person who gets the greatest lift out of the picture is the artist who paints it. He knows how it is done. Finding out how it is done becomes our next concern.

III

How a Prayer Group Lives and Dies

THE BIRTH OF A PRAYER GROUP

Since a cell is a friendship of spirits it is not called together as a committee meeting, and since it is a live organism it cannot be artificially started. A prayer group comes into being because it is called forth by a need in the lives of those who make it up. In a small gathering of group leaders the question was asked, "How did your cell begin?" Various answers were given. One grew out of a ministerial supply committee in a small New Hampshire Community Church; another had as its nucleus a study group for young parents; still another began when an emergency brought a group of friends together for intercessory prayer; another arose out of the prayer of one of its members for a prayer companion; and the last rooted out of one man's discouragement about his spiritual life and his coming to his pastor for help. Still another beginning was in answer by several individuals to a public announcement in a church paper or from the pulpit for those who were interested in prayer groups to come together to explore the idea. Special meetings are sometimes held at which a guest speaker introduces the plan of small prayer companies in the larger fellowship of the church.

One church that is having an outstanding success in the number and quality of its groups uses the following procedure: the minister serves as the convenor, calling together persons who he knows are interested in spiritual growth through prayer. He does not depend altogether on public announcement but also goes directly to individuals. Each is told of the purpose of the cell, the requirements as to weekly attendance, and the general group discipline. The

31

hoped-for result for each group started is a deepening of individual life, a new understanding of the Christian faith, and a willingness to experiment in thought and deed in putting into practice what each learns of God's will for himself. This practice of fluidity is essential from the very beginning. One of the vital rules for starting an atom is never, consciously or unconsciously, to lay down a law or to run it by any individual's preconceived ideas. Each prayer cell is an experiment in life much in the same sense that a child is an experiment. A mother who autocratically orders the life of her child either kills the child's spirit or loses it entirely. Jesus, whose stature as the Son of God gave him the *right* to direct, blended discipline with freedom. He permitted his disciples to make mistakes.

Actually it takes only one person to start a prayer group—a man, woman or young person filled with conviction and devotion. That person does not need leadership qualities; his only essential attribute is a contagion of spirit that will ignite another person. The first step is prayer. Pray for faith and love and keep on praying, and then pray that faith and love will possess those who will join in the fellowship of prayer. Cells have actually been born out of such prayer. One woman illustrates what has happened many times:

Six years ago I desperately and honestly wanted to know more about prayer. All my life I have tried to be a Christian, but I was weak in my prayer life. I had discovered through the years that the greatest power came to me when I prayed with others. I prayed for a prayer partner. A few days later a person whom I had met only once called me. After a short conversation we discovered we had a mutual desire, and we agreed to meet at a downtown church to study prayer. . . . We found new strength and discovered new insights, which we agreed to put into practice the following week. We met together each week for six weeks and then a third member came. I met her while shopping. As she expressed a desire to know more about prayer I invited her to join my friend and me.

This was the beginning of an interdenominational prayer cell of real significance to many lives.

Prayer is the first rule. The second is to seek those who you are led to believe are also seeking. Yield to guidance of the Spirit at this point and do not be held back by self-consciousness. Irving Harris, who is one of the leaders of the Calvary Church, New York, groups, began his own prayer cell with the building superintendent. He simply asked the superintendent to pray with him. Through joint prayer they discovered that they were brothers and needed to get together soon again. They each thought of one or two others to meet with them. As Mr. Harris puts it, "This man and I made a good team, and except for God-given initiative we would never have come together."

Church leaders have made use of their need for spiritual strength to draw their committees or Sunday school classes into the study and practice of prayer. One Sunday school teacher suddenly became aware that she had grown very little in twenty years. Very humbly she confessed this to her class of young married people. They too were led to an examination of their own devotional living and as a result asked the minister to form with them a prayer group where they could come for conversation, discussion and study about prayer. Out of these exploratory meetings they learned to pray and grow together.

Another group of sixteen women was the outgrowth of the feeling of a pastor's wife that she wanted a prayer partner. She began casually to pray with her neighbor and the fellowship was so rich that others joined them. For many years this group has been the soul of the church. Just as casually, a mixed cell was started over a coffeepot when one couple invited another couple to join them for coffee and prayer. The mutual spiritual questing in which these four engaged attracted eight other seekers.

In another case a minister's wife attended a training session for prayer group leadership. Inspired by the experience she invited three or four women in her own parish to join her in forming a group. Her husband, the minister, was so impressed that he issued a general invitation to his men's groups, and as usually happens, no one responded. He then personally invited the husbands of the women in his wife's prayer group. They accepted and now the men meet together.

Rules for beginning a spiritual atom may be summarized as follows:

Pray!

Take time to discover other members!

Follow all the light you can get—from minister, books, training conferences!

Begin simply with sincerity of commitment and leave the results to God!

WHO MAKES UP THIS PRAYER GROUP?

Cells are open to all ages and to both men and women. A family-like prayer group may be composed of persons of varying ages. Since the needs of youth and age are so different, however, a division according to age is usually preferable. If a mixed group becomes predominantly women, it often will be wise to begin a men's group, even though the number may be small.

More important than sex or age is the commitment of the members. Only a person with a seeking spirit becomes a genuine member of a fellowship group. This means that people who are self-satisfied, content with the status quo of the Church and the world about them, will not join a prayer group. "I don't need prayer," a woman said one time. "When I face a crisis, then I'll be willing to join a group."

Others may join at first because they think it is an expected thing to do. Such persons, however, either will eliminate themselves rather quickly, or will be so challenged intellectually and spiritually by the group's expectation of them to grow that they will become true seekers. For only those persons willing to grow, accepting with equal devotion the commitment of the group to its purpose, will continue in its membership.

WHERE AND WHEN DOES THE PRAYER GROUP MEET?

Most cells meet in the homes of the members. Such places of meeting afford a good sense of fellowship and going from home to home stretches the spiritual friendliness between members as well as blesses their dwellings with prayer. On the other hand, meeting in one place continuously for many weeks and months makes of it a sacred spot and there will be established an atmosphere of prayer and a sense of familiarity that will be of definite help to the group itself. When a home is used, a room large enough to avoid crowding and free from interruptions should be sought. It is desirable for the members to be able to dispose of their wraps before entering the meeting room, so that the quiet of the worship period is not broken into.

When prayer groups meet in churches, several places may be appropriate. The sanctuary may well serve for the period of worship and even for the full period of the intercessory group; but it is preferable to use a smaller room for the period of sharing, study or planning. Small chapels are of course ideal for the worship period and many of them across the country have become holy spots for those who have experienced the Presence of God within them. The group sense of His nearness seems to carry over from week to week.

A chapel is certainly not requisite. A worship center has been made in classrooms, small unused upper rooms, ministers' studies. In one church a group merely sat around Sunday school tables in a small classroom. The place makes little difference so long as there is adequate space, heat, light and privacy.

Many successful men's cells have been carried on in places of business. For years a men's group has met in a downtown office at eight-thirty on Friday mornings. Another is held in a central mid-town office where men have sandwiches brought in each Thursday and then spend forty-five minutes in prayer and sharing. From New Mexico comes this report of the beginning of one such atom for laymen:

The men met in the Franciscan Hotel at eight-thirty in the evening. Of the seven invited six arrived and the seventh phoned that he was ill. Every man present felt a Power and caught part of a vision of the meaning and possibility of working together as a cell. The only minister invited added much, but there was a freedom and a spontaneity about the conversation that was thrilling, after a brief time at the start in which every man prayed aloud and asked God's leading for the meeting. It was exciting, and the eagerness and obvious hunger on the part of each one for just such Christian fellowship made each man realize that the world is hungry for religion that works and fellowship that is real.

Probably the best known of all groups for men meets several days a week in a railroad car in Grand Central Station in New York.

WHEN THE PRAYER GROUP MEETS FOR THE FIRST TIME

No group will have its first meeting without the members having been given some preparation. If the group is called by invitation the person who extends it will obviously serve as convenor, though later any one of the group can carry out this function. These groups that have come together for a specific purpose, whether it is intercession, sharing or any other of the activities discussed in Chapter II, find it fairly easy to get under way. The first meeting may be a full-scale beginning of the regular program with the leader suggesting and carrying out a plan of procedure that has already been explained to all and approved. This is the form more fully explained in Part Two of this book.

On the other hand, those groups that begin without a clear pattern in mind will have to devote at least the first meeting and perhaps several to determining the exact purpose and the ensuing pattern they desire. In this case it will be the task of the leader to state the possible forms for the group and, perhaps, even to suggest a tentative pattern. It has often proven wise, however, before any pattern is suggested, for the fellowship to give every member an opportunity to tell his spiritual autobiography and to indicate his needs and interests. Brief autobiographies can be given in one or two meetings, this exchange leading into an actual discussion of what each may hope to receive from the group and thus of the form that it should take. The spirit of freedom should be maintained for some weeks (and indeed even throughout the whole life of the group), because needs will change, this often making advisable changes in pattern as well.

THE LEADER

Who are qualified to lead prayer cells? When a person attains genuine spiritual stature his wisdom is spontaneously recognized and direction is naturally asked of him. He becomes the leader. But these persons are rare. Just as rare are those groups that have no leaders, cells that have attained such maturity that if a stranger were to look in upon them he could not discover who was directing the group because all were participating. This situation involves a magnificent unity of spirit. As one white minister speaking in a Negro church observed, "I felt that if I were to stop my sermon at any point a dozen people could rise up immediately in the congregation and carry on without hesitation." This equal involvement of all in the affairs of the cell is a pattern followed in Friends' meetings for business and worship.

There must be, however, as much leadership as is essential. If it is unhealthy for one person to dominate a meeting or to have all of the members become dependent upon him, it is equally unhealthy for the group not to be given enough direction to prevent wasteful anarchy. If a prayer group has its purpose clearly defined, its members committed to that purpose, and a helmsman to steer it for a time until it gets out of the bay, then carried along by the Spirit, it is soon sailing a straight course. Otherwise its progress is spasmodic and uncertain as it is blown about by the caprices of its members, sometimes getting foundered before it starts. The varying interests of an unwelded set of people are apt to loom up as goals and confusion set in. Then too, a bewildered group of people is a field ripe for persons who have a tendency to dominate. Since there are usually more than one of these, competition is added to the other difficulties. A leader acceptable to all is a requisite for the beginning of such groups.

Such a leader will first of all be willing on the one hand to use all his skills and abilities when they are needed, and on the other hand to strive to create a situation in which his direction is unnecessary. From the very beginning the director makes it clear that his position is temporary and that the group will soon come to the stage where any one of them can serve as moderator. The participation of a leader should be the minimum necessary to give direction to the meeting. He keeps the discussion within the limits agreed upon, gently controls those who speak too long, consistently draws out those who are shy and hesitant. One of the joys of those who lead cells is to realize that this restraint and encouragement soon are not needed, that the fellowship has become real.

All groups profit by having a moderator. Or as one person puts it, someone to break the silence. This role may well be rotated, regardless of the nature of the group. Yet most mature groups leave the simple task of unifying the meetings in the hands of one person, since nothing can be gained by passing the responsibility from person to person. Special study groups, of course, are benefited by a teacher or director of studies. One meditation cell that has gone into a consideration of the various forms of prayer has had certain members lead those studies or has invited guests to conduct them.

A prayer group that follows the pattern described in Part Two of this book requires the leadership of a devoted person who may be either minister or layman. Experience in the weekly meetings, counseling with the members of the group, gleaning ever new insights through intensive reading of books on prayer and the devotional life—all these help fit him for such leadership. Such a director will practice himself every discipline provided for the group and will probably do much more for his spiritual development. He will read incessantly the devotional classics, the works on spiritual direction, and many volumes on prayer. He will listen closely to anyone who has suggestions to offer out of his own prayer experience, meager or wide though this may be. He will listen humbly to the sharing within his own group, for out of this will come helps for his own spirit as well as indications of the needs to be met in later meetings.

More than all else, he will keep most faithfully to his own daily quiet time. In the silence he will hold up regularly the members of his prayer cell to the love of God. There will be occasions when he will be blessed with insights so wonderful that for hours his soul will sing a song of thanksgiving. Hour after hour he will lift his heart quickly and simply to God with loving and humble phrases. He will yield himself so wholeheartedly to every whispering of the Spirit that his day will be zestful and alive. He will know what the exiles meant when they said after their return: "When the Lord turned again the captivity of Zion, we were like them that dream. Then was our mouth filled with laughter, and our tongue with singing: then said they among the heathen, The Lord hath done great things for them." (Psalms 126:1–2.)

Can cell leaders get training? The Laymen's Movement for a Christian World, Rye, New York, and the Kirkridge Retreat Center, Bangor, Pennsylvania, have in recent years been conducting a series of retreat-conferences for leaders of prayer groups. These gatherings of several days' duration vary in procedure and program, but the general outline includes a consideration of the purpose and method of prayer group leadership, an inquiry into the values and practice of intercessory and interior prayer, a study of the Bible and of devotional classics that are suitable for those interested in spiritual growth. These conferences are carried through in the atmosphere of a retreat with much silence and time for individual study. They combine to a remarkable degree demonstration and teaching with a genuine cell experience for those attending.

PRAYER GROUP DISCIPLINE

History has not been moved by disembodied ideals but by small groups that discipline themselves to live out in all sorts of environments the ideology they have accepted—to bring heaven to earth, so to speak. The Third Order of St. Francis was lifted out of the realm of emotional aspiration into an effective way of life among men by a common discipline that trained the participants for such living. Cells pass from "the fervor of the novice" whenever they set for themselves a discipline and attempt sincerely to live by it day by day. A discipline lifts wishful thinking about goodness into the actual life of goodness. Thus, a rule of life serves both as a means to growth and as a standard for checking conduct.

A discipline as an individual concern is more difficult to observe than a common rule of life. Here the cell is most valuable. The bond of a mutual obligation is a great strengthener even for the strongest. A beginning group can rejoice when it comes to the solid ground of working out a common way of life. It means that the members are secure enough with one another to expect one another to live by a standard that they themselves expect to live by.

As indicated earlier some groups come together expecting to accept a cell discipline already formulated. Others soon discover the necessity of shaping a rule of life by which the members may best grow. Growth together is essential if fellowship is to be formed or maintained. This group discipline may have various expressions, but whatever its content may be, if it is to be forceful in the lives of its makers, it will grow out of their conscious needs and will be subject to change as the need arises. Common rules usually grow out of an effort to implement the most pertinent Christian teachings.

Jesus' words, "Follow me," are an eternal call to discipleship. When we who aspire to be his disciples are living in the Holy Spirit which Jesus' life and death released into the world, our lives are carried on in perfect obedience to his call and to all the precepts he gave to his first disciples. Most of us have not grown in the Spirit as we should and it is for the purpose of coming to our full stature in Christ that we come together in cell groups. Thus the best discipline that we can devise flows from Christ's teachings. Whatever resistance there is to the idea of an ordered life melts away in the light of such a glorious manifestation of goodness as Jesus revealed among men. No one practices a rule of life because he thinks he can make himself holy. The work of any seeker is to possess his own will that he may surrender it to the Divine will. It is in this complete surrender that he acquires true goodness. But he cannot give up his will unless he possesses it. If his will is untrained he is a victim of every whim and desire of mind and body. Hence, it is to free himself for growth that he employs a discipline.

One basic rule of all groups is required attendance. God expects His children to return to Him with their whole hearts; therefore, those activities that speed that return must have high priority. Only earnest, committed people should join a prayer group, and a willingness to attend the meetings regularly is one small indication of this devotion.

A second rule is that the members are expected to carry on their private devotional life every day. Attendance at the meeting will do no more to deepen the life of the spirit than will attendance at a weekly church service unless the intent of the meeting is carried over into daily living. A very general practice of groups is to expect their members to have a period of prayer each day and frequently it is understood that each member will hold all the other members up into the Light of God during that prayer period. "Let us begin this practice of the Presence of God," says Brother Lawrence, "and help one another with our prayers."

Beyond these two minimum disciplines a group is free to go as far as it wishes or is led. One group spent several months discussing the values of life, the principles for implementing those values, and a set of rules for making those principles concrete. The members later realized that those months when they clarified their purposes and attempted definite means to accomplish them were the most worth-while periods of its existence. From their mutual exploration twelve cardinal goals of life emerged: the love of God, the love of man, humility, truthfulness, unqualified commitment, joyousness, fearlessness, equanimity, control of the body, simplicity, right livelihood and group loyalty. The rules that followed included: daily half-hour periods of worship and prayer, nonviolence in thought, word and deed, and honesty in all one's dealings.

The Quaker practice is to couch the discipline in query form. Eight young men who banded themselves together during their camp experience in World War II used *The Imitation of Christ* as a guidebook. They drew from it certain queries by which they examined themselves both corporately and individually. The query would be read, and then in searching silence, in sharing aloud, and sometimes in writing an honest answer, they helped one another to grow.

A tentative discipline was formulated by a cell that feared the deadening effect of a strict set of rules. It entitled its suggestions as to a way of life as, "Some Things We Might Do":

> Come regularly.
> Be on time for the quiet period.
> Set aside half an hour each day to
> > pray,
> > read the best things,
> > listen to the best music,
> > write down the best thoughts.
> To talk to one person a week about prayer.

In time this simple set of suggestions became their discipline.

Two disciplined movements have come into being within the free churches in the past decade as an expression of this need in the religious life. One is the Disciplined Order of Christ, under the leadership of Albert E. Day; the other is the Kirkridge Fellowship, under the direction of John Oliver Nelson. The discipline of each is included.

The Disciplined Order of Christ requires six duties of its members:

1. To seek for ourselves the highest New Testament standard of Christian experience and life;
2. To seek to promote the highest New Testament standard of Christian experience and life among others;
3. To seek first the Kingdom of God, not in our lives merely, but in the life of the world;
4. To acknowledge the praying and witnessing church, wherever it exists in the Body of Christ;
5. To be guided in the meaning and fulfillment of these duties by a recognition of the validity and authority of centuries of Christian experience, especially with their universal testimony; and
6. To support and advance the Disciplined Order of Christ by earnest prayer and an annual sacrificial gift.

The Kirkridge Fellowship is a Christian group with a retreat center near Bangor, Pennsylvania. The center and the movement were inspired by the Iona Community of Scotland, which has done much to revivify the church life of that country. The Fellowship in this country has both a set of rules and a series of intentions. These are fairly exacting, but they are accepted by ministers and lay people all over the country. A quarterly accounting is expected of all members. The rules follow:

1. To keep a daily half hour of devotion before 9:00 A.M. (or at another regular hour);
2. To read the agreed lectionary and use the agreed hymns;
3. To pray at the day's end;
4. To offer grace at each meal;
5. To make a personal retreat each month;
6. To tithe consistently;
7. To work for the growth of a Christian cell where I am;
8. To share corporate church worship weekly, and an interchurch activity quarterly;
9. To make a retreat with other Kirkridge members once yearly.

The lectionary mentioned in Rule 2 includes the reading of the same Bible chapter each day for a week, and the memorizing of one hymn each month. In addition to the Rules there are eight Intentions:

1. To live frugally;
2. To identify myself with all those with whom Christ would have fellowship;
3. To demonstrate my Christianity in civic action;
4. To grow intellectually as a Christian;
5. To practice Christian reconciliation;
6. To share myself with my household;
7. To share my Christian faith and discovery with some new person each month;
8. To pray constantly.

In his book, *Alternative to Futility*, D. Elton Trueblood cites the prayer group movement as one of the signs of hope in these dark days, and states five principles of Christian living and five disciplines which might well be chosen by such groups:

Five Principles for Christian Living

1. Commitment—The acceptance of convictions by putting them into one's daily living.
2. Witness—Public witness to our faith, by word and action.
3. Fellowship—Group guidance in major decisions, and the authority of the group experience.
4. Vocation—Regardless of one's job, putting Christian faith to work actively: Christian carpenter, Christian teacher, Christian pupil, etc.
5. Discipline—Loyal acceptance of rules or discipline.

A Minimum Discipline

1. Worship—Regular sharing in public worship, a minimum of once a week.
2. Solitude—Agreement to spend part of each day alone for private prayer and devotional reading.
3. Silence—Getting the body and mind still, to listen to the voice of God; a minimum of fifteen minutes with an hour of silence the goal.

4. Love—The way of social concern for others, every day including some outgoing activity not for ourselves alone.
5. Austerity—Simple living, releasing the mind from worldly interests, and releasing the income for the service of God and man.

These principles and rules have been placed on pledge cards by some cells, with the notation, "It is my intention, with God's help, to live by the foregoing principles and to practice daily the above discipline." It is to be signed by the individual joining the prayer cell, then is to be returned to him after he becomes a member. Thus there is no accounting except to oneself and God. Each member is his own guardian, so to speak.

Yet another example of a discipline is that prepared by the Commission on Evangelism of the Evangelical and Reformed Church, to be used either by individuals or by groups. It has seven points:

1. Attend church regularly and practice the presence of God daily—without exception.
2. Read one chapter of the Bible each day, beginning with the New Testament, Matthew 1.
3. Approach all men and situations (good or evil) with a Christian attitude of sympathetic understanding, appreciation and positive helpfulness.
4. Strive for a will-to-believe that "all things work together for good to them that love God."
5. Pursue as the dominant ambition and purpose of life the attainment of "oneness with God in Christ" and the peace, strength and quality of soul that flow from it.
6. Believe in and seek community with "The Holy Catholic Church" —the Body of Christ.
7. Bear witness to the peace and power of God in the daily routine of life, through radiant living, marked by a spirit of joy and thanksgiving.

Each prayer group that wants something more than a minimum rule of life can either start afresh and have the worth-while experience of working out its own set of principles and disciplines or it can adopt and modify one of these sets that is already in existence. The group will find that it offers many values, not the least of which is the sense of purpose and unity that it gives to the life of the spirit as the members go about their daily activities.

PROBLEMS

Some children come into homes where they are so well-nurtured that they are not handicapped by any of the usual diseases that youngsters catch, such as whooping cough and measles. All, however, suffer more or less from growing pains. Some cells, too, may escape many difficulties, but none is free from the problem of growing, unless they die in infancy. A few of the common disadvantages and problems that assail most groups are considered below.

Visitors—Yes or No?

Visitors are both problems and joys just as in the ordinary family. Too many of them of the wrong kind can break up a family and no company at all can make the home life exceedingly dull. Much, of course, depends on the nature of the group and the phase of its existence. It often happens that the intimacy of the gathered meeting is broken (if it ever was achieved!) if an open-door policy is adopted in either a meditation or sharing cell. People reveal their deepest selves only in an atmosphere of trust and affection, this seldom being where strangers are. Some guests freeze the sharing at a superficial level. Others warm the air. It is extremely impractical, however, to examine every potential visitor to weigh his fellowship potential. Hence, the wise procedure when the group finds itself in a phase where the members are involved with deep inner problems is to make a rule forbidding visitors. Of course, intercessory groups are often strengthened by visitors, provided they are acquainted with the purpose of the meetings.

Aggressive visitors are still another difficulty at times. Such persons are inclined, perhaps unwittingly, to take the opportunity to give an address. Someone has said that whether he is a guest or a member, a person should never take more than ten minutes to hold forth in a cell meeting. (We believe that only at rare times, though, should anyone take even that long!) If the guest is a notable person, however, there is a tendency on the part of the group to ask him to speak, even though he may not desire to do so. A good policy for a small group (concentrating on meditation, sharing or study) to decide upon is that anyone who comes in is expected to fit into the life and program of the meeting, unless he has been invited beforehand to bring a special contribution. If this procedure is thoroughly understood by all the members, any caller will understand his role as a visitor.

New Members—When and How?

Growth is natural. Some groups grow faster than others, some encourage growth and others do not seek it. Yet all cells increase in numbers sooner or later if they are growing in spirit and the relationship between members is meaningful. Bishop Stephen Neill of the World Council of Churches said a cell *must* grow to remain a cell; otherwise, it bceomes a cyst. The usual questions are these: Should anyone be admitted? Should there be preliminary preparation? Should membership be open at all times? How should the newcomer be integrated into the program?

Each fellowship develops its own answers to these questions and the solutions vary according to the purpose of the cell. Just as it is easiest for the intercessory group to welcome visitors, so it is the most open to receive new members. About the only requirement is a faith in intercessory prayer and an acquaintance with the practices of the particular group. It has been discovered that the meditation group needs to exercise the greatest precaution in adding new members. A certain familiarity with the use of silence is essential, as well as an understanding of the way and its goal. The meditation cell is not intended for those who are eager to be part of a general fellowship or who are spiritually curious—and there are such. When the meaning and practice of interior prayer are not understood, the period of silence is not helpful. It is quite obvious too that not all persons can use interior prayer. The attempt to do so simply because someone else is using it profitably is a misapplication of one's spiritual talents. Such persons coming into a meditation group eventually eliminate themselves, but their presence in the cell will not have been altogether a happy experience.

A careful inquiry into the purposes, understanding and commitment of a prospective member is beneficial no matter what the type of cell. One meditation group proceeds most cautiously with potential members. At first, two regular members invite him to have luncheon with them, informing him about all the features of the cell. At the same time, as they get to know him, they learn of his background and interest. If they discover that he was not clear as to the purpose of the group but that he still evinces a desire to join, they then give him several study books to read, and invite him to visit a meeting of the fellowship. Then the three of them get together again, and if there is a mutual conviction that he is ready for the cell and the cell is ready for him, the prospective member is asked to attend several meetings to confirm the decision. This method allows him to drop out gracefully if on further association he feels that the cell does not meet his needs, or, if it does meet them, his trial status automatically becomes that of full membership.

One precedent to be established early in a group's life is this: do not retrace ground already covered in order to brief the new member. He can be geared to the ongoing program by his own desire to study and associate with individual members and by their openness to him at other times than the meeting time. The life of the spirit is a spiraling one, and those who are working at it are drawn to subjects already considered time and time again, but on a higher level than in earlier studies. Thus the one entering the cell benefits from the new insights that come. On the other hand, all group members have found that they benefit from the new member with his questions and with the fresh spiritual experiences that he brings.

When the Prayer Group Stagnates

Because growth is silent and spontaneous we do not pay too much attention to it. Yet sometimes there comes to us the realization that we are not changing. Perhaps it is someone on the outside who has to discover the sad fact that nothing is happening. One young minister going into a new parish commented on the group in his church as being exceedingly dull. New eyes on old groups might be helpful, for as Brother Lawrence says, "Not to go forward is to go backward." A group search for the Presence of God strengthens the individual members when they have their times of trouble—dryness, discouragement, losing of faith. The real problem arises when the group itself comes into these times of distress. Every group can expect to drop in its enthusiasm and to be discouraged, for cells have personalities of their own and cycles of mood.

If a cell is at a standstill, it should honestly face itself to discover its difficulty, raising all possible reasons for the dryness that has overtaken it. Some of the reasons for the slump may be as follows: the members have lost confidence in the validity of their prayer practices, or the cell has fulfilled the function for which it was created, or the members have come to the place where new commitments are to be made, which they are tempted to avoid, or the group as a whole has become too introspective. Whatever the reasons, the time of examination is at hand.

If it is the method of prayer that is causing the lack of zest for the cell, a study and comparison of other methods will help reveal the situation. It is possible, however, that such reading will reveal that the group has stopped growing or being effective because it has reached the limit of the commitment of its members. Whenever an individual or a group holds back from giving all to God, he or it is unable to receive all that God is offering. When this is seen, and reservations and negativity are set aside, the whole scene is changed and the path becomes clear again.

When a fellowship has completed the concern that brought it together in the first place, there is no more need to continue. If a work project is completed, if a sharing group has probed as far into its individual problems as it can go, if a study group has finished its study, it is obvious that there is no more to do. Yet it is strange that many times a group is unaware of what has happened. Taking up a new emphasis is the simplest answer to this problem: the sharing group undertakes a study, the study group undertakes a project, the workout group becomes an intercessory or a meditation group.

Discouragement may come because results seem negligible. Intercessory prayer groups, praying for world peace, may become discouraged because the world scene remains unchanged, or because it decides the crisis is past. A meditation group may be disappointed because apparently little change takes place in the lives of those participating. Says Allan Hunter:

Don't be discouraged, the headlines may be just the same. You can't be in a cell and fulfill the conditions which your team-mates will work out in new ways, without having something terribly significant come out of the cooperation. Not just flashes of unexpected insight—that will happen at practically every meeting—but something more important, which is far more important, which is far more personal than you guessed—the sense of belonging, of being made not for time, but for that which is beyond time.

Meditation and sharing groups are apt to go stale because of self-interest, or too much in-looking and not enough out-reaching. It is inevitable that in the beginning of a prayer cell, because of the sudden awareness of one's own inadequacy in the light of the holiness of God, one's entire thought centers upon self. There is puzzlement in the revelation of oneself, so different are we from what we thought we were; but there is also delight in the growing awareness of the Presence of God. We do not readily want to turn from our puzzlement and our delight, since both of them speak to the self. At first we want to know about ourselves and God, and we are not bothered in thinking of others.

But to think of oneself is the way to destruction. To avoid death through selfhood, we must turn from self to others. Still searching for His will for ourselves we find ourselves coming into a joyous relationship with His other children. An ingrown, introspective cell may recover its health again if it plunges into some worth-while service project.

Whatever may be the cause of the stunted development of the cell, there is power in the individuals, or maybe in one individual, to rescue it and start it on the creative path again. If some member has courage to take a creative step forward, the chances are he can kindle others to begin living again. Deeper commitment on the part of one carries forward the whole.

The Troublesome Member—How Does He Change?

The most painful and frustrating problem a prayer group faces may center around one individual. Usually he does one of two things (or both of them!): he has a passion to dominate the group, or he brings all his troubles and spreads them before the group week after week. The group needs to know that both of these manifestations have the same root. These individuals are lonely people, the group probably offering them the most satisfying relationship they have. If a cell is strong enough to make a creative response to the challenge such persons offer, it is possible to transform both the individuals involved and the members of the group themselves.

Our culture creates these troublesome persons and unwittingly we contribute to their isolation and unloveableness. Hence we have a responsibility to relieve their unhappiness. Careful consideration and preparation before a group starts, or a member is admitted, often will prevent the problem arising or will help individuals to grow. Most people who are not willing to grow will eliminate themselves. If the troublesome person is established in the group, however, the creative response demands patience, gentleness, love and firmness. Firmness is as essential as the other virtues. Firmness is required to protect the group from becoming the victim of the troublesome person, and gentleness and patience are required to win him to more healthy ways of finding relationship. It is a mistake summarily to exclude any person from the cell. The choice of his association with it should always be left open so that he can respond creatively to the group.

The following plan has been used successfully. The first step is an indirect effort on the part of the leader to make it clear that no one person is to speak too long and that everyone is to participate. A successful leader finds ways to interrupt one who persists in talking too long, such as directing discussion to someone else. He says simply, "Yes, George, I agree completely with the point you are making, but Ruth hasn't expressed herself as yet. Ruth, what do you feel about it?" Sometimes he must be blunt, and say, "Now, George, you've had the floor long enough. Let's give someone else a chance." If such indirect suggestions fail, then a group of two or three have a meeting with him. This conference is carried on in prayer and with respect for the troublesome person; yet nevertheless it raises the issue clearly. In most extreme cases the question may need to be raised as to whether or not the individual feels that the group is the proper one for him. The choice of leaving the group or facing the problem creatively should always be left open for his own decision. If such a procedure fails to bring the right response, the group then confers with George about his failing and urges upon him the necessity of facing it. This method requires love and sympathetic understanding as well as a degree of self-criticism on the part of every member of the group. The corporate approach to his problem can be of inestimable value.

In instances when it is obvious that the troublesome person is in need of psychological help, the group members should take responsibility for helping their friend to get that assistance. Psychotherapeutic groups are now in existence in which neurotic persons may find an answer to their problems. If none exists near at hand the fostering of such a group may be the project that will be a fitting expression to the prayer life of the cell. Pastor and laymen have accomplished much as they worked together with those psychotherapeutic agencies available in their communities.

Many stories could be told of lives that have been changed when a group has dealt creatively with a troublesome person. To be accepted and loved has often of itself been sufficient to change the person and remove from him the need for more than his share of attention and relate him in such a way that he was able to make his creative contribution to the lives of his fellow seekers. Whenever this happens the group itself has been enriched and when mistakes have been made and even failure has been the outcome, the group itself has learned where it did not live up to its highest guidance. Somehow life manages to let us correct our mistakes, and once having failed, the cell that is sincere will find a better answer the next time.

Dissensions—a Sign of Immaturity

Disagreeing people are apt to stay in two camps unless there is a third alternative that lifts them higher than either contention would. If the purpose of the cell is clear and has the loyal commitment of the group, controversies can be avoided by constantly returning to that purpose. If we are searching for the rich jewels of God, we will not be detained long by a common stone that we have picked up along the way. Difficult questions, however, are not always to be avoided. They are to be faced objectively in the light of Christ's teachings and in that light to be worked through.

In spite of this knowledge that is accepted in all cells, it does happen that at times discussion gets emotionally charged and tension begins to disintegrate the spirit of the group. Most people will yield to the suggestion that the subject be dropped temporarily and discussed elsewhere when there is time to give the disagreeing persons unhurried attention. It is at this point that the maturity of the leader to make an unbiased objective act really counts. Any person who is free from fear and self-importance, and is not opinionated—in other words is a channel of the Holy Spirit—can unite the dissenting members who have full confidence in him and his judgment. Any person dominated by an outgoing love for God and man can bring a group back to an objective point of view. Silence is a powerful unifying agent. Praying in silence softens the hardness and restores the spirit. When moments of dissension arise, the leader need not be anxious if he can achieve a prayerful silence. Such a hush invites the Holy Spirit to alter the situation. The Friends' meeting for business furnishes many examples of this miracle. When Friends are divided some Friend will ask for silence. Out of this period of worship there usually emerges a creative third solution upon which minds meet easily.

When the Group Grows Too Large

Twelve is the optimum number. When the group gets above this, the time has come to change the form of the cell. The obvious way is to form a new group and this is the simplest solution, providing the old group has developed leadership. One meditation group establishes beginners' groups which have a short period of silence and a great deal of study of the works on interior prayer. These beginners' cells either form meditation cells, or unite with cells already in existence.

A second method of meeting this problem brought by growth is to subdivide into two groups. This, as has been pointed out, is the method of the biological cell: indefinite subdivision until there are many cells. Theoretically this is a simple step, but actually it has proven to be a very difficult one. What is the basis for such division when the cell has been a vital one and all the members desire to stay together? The way of meeting the problem becomes really practical only when a natural method of division suggests itself. The interests among the five activities to be discussed later in detail, or in the type of study pursued, may serve as the dividing line.

If the fellowship has become close-knit and there is a question about adequate leadership to fulfill either of the above plans, a third solution has been carried out successfully. In this plan, the entire group continues to meet together for the period of worship. After this a division into two or three smaller groups takes place for closer fellowship and study. Division of the cell is not an easy process but the advantages of the small intimate group outweigh the difficulty.

The Life of the Prayer Group

When does a cell outlive its usefulness? The age of a cell does not necessarily measure its success. Some groups have existed only a year or two and in that time have served a vital purpose; others have been in existence for many years and are far beyond the time of their highest value. The first seven weeks are crucial for a beginning atom. If the group has gained sufficient power to carry into its third month, it will most likely go on as a center of strength in the spiritual life. Many groups do not carry through this period, usually because of inadequate leadership or lack of concern on the part of those in the group.

There are two good reasons why fellowship groups come to an end. The most common reason is American mobility; for example, the college class is graduated and the students scatter, or a husband gets a new job in another city and a vital family moves away. If the nucleus of the fellowship is left, a new beginning is made. Indeed, if only one interested person is left in a community, that can be enough.

The other reason why a group may end is simply that the cell will have served its purpose—lived out its life, so to speak. To recognize that the job is completed is much more healthy than to permit that which has been alive and useful to wither away. So long as members are committed, a company of spiritual seekers may go on for many years and experience many mountain peaks of rich fellowship, both human and Divine. Yet the time may and does come when it would be wise to recognize that the disbanding of the group is the guided course.

Even though the life of the group is of only a few months' duration, it is still a worth-while experience. Every effort in the search for God contributes to the sum total of man's seeking and expecting and helps open the way for a new breakthrough of the Holy Spirit. When we have tried every way we know and after much prayer it has become clear that the fellowship has served its purpose, let us gently and lovingly lay it down. Any company that has been together in the Presence of God, seeking together to live a new kind of life, giving themselves more deeply to one another and to God, has furthered the love of God in the world! No cell, after all, is an isolated bit of life. Each is a light on the altar that testifies to the power of faith and fellowship to transform lives. John Haynes Holmes describes cells thus: "Little communities of sanctified souls, their membership anonymous—have never died out. They burn the lights before the altar that is to bring back the day after the long, cold night."

IV

The Meditation Group

Robert Barclay, looking in on a company of seventeenth-century Seekers, described them thus: "When I came into the silent assemblies of God's people, I felt a secret power among them which touched my heart; and as I gave way to it, I found the evil weakening in me and the good raised up." The observation of the ancient Friend well explains the work of modern meditation cells.

Meditation is a term with a wide variety of meanings. It is used here to indicate that form of prayer in which the self is brought before God and offered to Him: an act of openness to the Holy Spirit. Interior prayer is commonly considered a solitary work and each person who would come to the deep levels of his own being and to a oneness with God does seemingly make a solitary pilgrimage. Yet no one travels alone. Gerald Heard, modern-day exponent of the practice of the Presence of God, says,

It is clear no individual can stand by himself against the invincible ignorance and the blind beliefs in greed and fear as the only social forces which still dominate our society today. He must gain practical actual reassurance that this belief is only a deadly half-truth which vanishes when the light of actual devotion is kindled against it. He can, however, no more do this by himself than a traveller who has tumbled into a bog in the dark can strike a light to see his way out. His matches are damp. Only in the group-field of fellow believers can he rekindle his light. That, however, is only half a truth. History shows that small groups meeting once a week for meditation, if each member is every day meditating by himself (and by meditation is meant the spiritual exercise every sincerely religious mind recognizes as essential to the spirit) do have an experience of precipitated power. This is not only uniquely restorative, bodily as well as mentally, not only makes the members capable of real cooperative behavior and unlimited liability

55

toward each other, but also gives each a power to deal generously and with creative initiative with all outside.[1]

Heard then goes on to state that the effectiveness of such a field depends upon (1) the degree of unity the members have as to the goal; (2) the faith they have in dynamic affection; (3) the degree to which they have learned to meditate and use silence; and (4) the degree to which they maintain regular periods of meditation each day.

Silence is the predominant active characteristic of meditation groups, although it cannot wisely be omitted from any cell. An uninformed observer might remark at first glance, "What is happening? What is the meaning of sitting still, and saying nothing?" Yet in the silence miracles may and do happen. Central to the life of any prayer fellowship is the shared worship in the silence. The real meaning of the corporateness becomes manifest in the sense of genuine mutual relationship with God. In the merged awareness of the divine-human connection there comes amazing fellowship. As Thomas Kelly puts it: "They [members of the blessed community] get at one another through Him. He is actively moving in all, co-ordinating those who are pliant to His will. . . . In glad amazement and wonder we enter upon a relationship which we had not known the world contained for the sons of men." [2]

As Jesus stated it, "Where two or three are gathered together in my name, there am I in the midst of them." This undoubtedly was the central experience of early Christian groups as well as of all Seeker groups. It is a corporate experience of the inflow of the Holy Spirit. The power lies in a group becoming aware of the uniting power of the Divine Spirit integrating personalities within themselves and at the same time setting up a line of generous communication between individuals. Something unaccountable happens in the silence of people who are simply opening themselves to the "breeze of the Spirit" or, using the Friendly term, "centering down."

The procedure of interior prayer is comparatively unknown among

[1] Gerald Heard, as quoted in *Cells for Peace* by Douglas Steere. Pamphlet, Fellowship of Reconciliation, New York, 1947.

[2] Thomas Kelly: *A Testament of Devotion* (New York: Harper & Brothers, 1941), pp. 83, 77.

Protestant groups. Each year, however, modern studies are written and invaluable devotional classics are put into circulation. These constitute the basis of study for meditation groups. A full bibliography can be found in Appendix I of this volume.

Meditation groups are among the longest-lived, two present-day groups being over twelve years old. The one described below is in a large city and is made up of professional men and women of various faiths. This particular company of seekers spends three hours together weekly, praying silently, reading devotional literature and studying techniques of spiritual growth.

A few years ago there came to me [writes the founder of the cell] a new realization of what prayer is. A wise and gifted man of God helped me to see how much fuller life could be with the spiritual dimension added. He introduced me to four others who were also beginning to take prayer seriously. Before long we decided to meet once a week in a nearby meeting house for an hour's shared meditation, Monday afternoon after office hours, 5:30-6:30. From the beginning the hour was kept in silence. The same room was used for ten years, and we always sat in an elongated circle to accommodate our growing fellowship. Chimes in a nearby clock regularly reminded us when the hour was at an end. Our benediction was a circle of clasped hands. Inevitably the group has grown and includes both men and women. The nearby apartment of one of the first women members has influenced the group. Early we found that to pray together was not enough. We needed to talk over mutual problems—share books.

One of our members for a number of years prepared a simple supper ahead of time so that when we gathered together after the hour's meditation, we were soon seated, trays on laps, partaking of a common meal. One member reads aloud a book on prayer or the spiritual life. Except for reading the meal is in silence. The third and last hour is given over to discussion and sharing.[3]

Out of the experience of this meditation group some pertinent helps have evolved.

During the half-hour, or better still, the hour preceding the meditation, you should not be hurried or fretful. Try to keep your mind from getting distracted by annoyances, anger, or anxiety. If you are physically

[3] Prayer Groups, Woman's Division of Christian Service, the Methodist Church.

fatigued try to get some rest and relaxation, perhaps a nap, during the afternoon. Try to come to the prayer group with a rested and relaxed mind, body and spirit.

Start the meditation period itself with vocal prayer [that is, silent and intent repetition of worded prayers by which attention is focussed]. Ask God's forgiveness for the sins you have committed. Offer them up to Him as they may occur to you while your mind dwells honestly over the events of the past hours. Tell Him that you are weak and hopeless without His mercy and help. Do not chide nor condemn yourself for your wrongdoings—just offer up your failures and ask for more strength to meet your next testings, and more love for God and all whom you are placed with.

After asking for forgiveness and praying for God's help in the hours and days ahead, turn to pray for individuals whom you are concerned about. Hold these persons in the Light. Hold them in Love toward God, that is, think of them as being surrounded by God's loving care and His desire to claim them to Himself. If it seems right for you to pray for a special blessing, such as health, always ask for it only if it is God's will and if it will lead to growth in spirit. All intercessory prayer should be given simply, not demandingly, and as soon as given, be offered up—be put trustingly in God's hands.

Then move to praise and adoration of God. Here, memorized prayers help. Sometimes you can thank God for special blessings, such as the supreme one of giving us this life as a period of time in which to grow to be more and more in His image and likeness. Thank Him for Himself, that He gives purpose and meaning and joy to existence. Thank Him for others who have also been given the desire to grow toward union with Him.

Such praying sometimes leads to the prayer of Quiet [sitting quietly, without movement of body, or word of mouth or mind] to look toward Him who is all Purity and Love and Peace. This is to hold ourselves unhurriedly in His presence. Sooner or later we will find that some distracting thought or picture has flitted into our consciousness; then we should attempt, as masters of prayer say, "to look over its shoulder," not to try to stamp it down but ignore it. We look again toward God with a little prayer that He help us toward Him.

If, however, this loving direction of your will toward God cannot easily be maintained, do not condemn yourself. Realize again that you are not to hurry or strain after the desired goal. Recall some hymn and let it sing inwardly to increase your devotion. Recall some idea from your recent reading and meditate on it. Ask yourself to be reminded of some scriptural passage that now needs the inner interpretations that the Holy Spirit can give.

Remember always that God leads us in our praying as in every activity if we learn more and more to ask His leading and to trust His guiding hand.[4]

As members of the meditation group work together they will inevitably grow in the art of sharing and the work of loving intercession. We shall now turn our attention to cells which major in these areas.

[4] Prayer Groups, Woman's Division of Christian Service, the Methodist Church.

V

The Sharing Group

A description of the meeting between Saint Louis and the poor Franciscan, Giles, sets forth the essence of the sharing group. Once Saint Louis, dressed as a poor pilgrim, knocked on the plain door of the simple Franciscan monastery. Giles, the doorkeeper, ran to meet the guest. They embraced and knelt together in silence. Then, without breaking the silence, Louis arose and went his way. Later when Giles joined the company of the other monks, they all set up a clamor because he had exchanged no words with the visitor. With fine simplicity Giles answered, "I read his heart and he read mine."

"I read his heart and he read mine" is no unusual experience for members of a prayer fellowship. As closeness grows between people, they know where words come from. Openness of heart is sharing.

Sharing is a necessary element in every cell. When it becomes the prime activity of a group, the group is a sharing cell. A sharing group may later become a meditation or an intercessory group at various stages just as either of these may develop into a sharing group.

The seeker is led into more perfect obedience to the first half of the Great Commandment by the meditation facet of cell life. The sharing factor leads him into obedience to the second half of this commandment. An ever-widening school of psychotherapy declares with increasing emphasis that interpersonal relatedness is the important thing. The travesty of men and nations has come about because the lines of communication are down. Devastating Iron Curtains are real not only between nations but also between persons. We need no psychological researchers to tell us that each of us needs to be with people we like and who like us, near enough to them to talk to them and to be talked to by them on a deep level. Such interchange with people who care integrates our fragmented lives. Beyond this, however, we need to be useful to others and have them be useful to us. The great tragedy for any one of us is to be told, whether vocally or by implication, "We don't need you."

The sharing group meets these patent needs of the lonely person. Once satisfactory relationships on a deep level are made, grounds are laid for other relationships.

Once a young woman complained to her minister about the cold and unfriendly people with whom she rode to work each morning. "Are all people unfeeling like that? They don't seem to care!" Ten weeks later she said to her pastor, "Has the world changed?" "Changed in what way?" he asked. "Are people more friendly than they used to be?" she continued. "Why, when I get on the bus to go to work, everybody smiles and we laugh and talk all the way in. The world didn't use to be like that." Weeks later she discovered that the change was in herself, and she exclaimed in wonderment, "Did I change that much?"

Sharing *per se* is not holy. Sharing can resemble in many ways a gossiping tea party, the only difference being that the subject is oneself instead of one's neighbors. Two elements lift sharing onto holy ground—love for God and man, and a sincere desire to grow in that love. The fundamental basis of sharing on a deep level is love. By love we do not mean sentimentality. To be loving, as we have said before, means respect for another's personality, a sense of responsibility and concern for another's welfare, and a desire for the growth of that person. A sharing cell is alive when it has in it persons who desire to love and be loved in this manner. Willingness to cultivate an understanding spirit plus a forgiving spirit is the creative atmosphere in which sharing blossoms into the flower of good living.

What Does the Group Share?

The members may share their faith in the fundamental practices of religion. This is the story of one cell, made up of mature seekers, all of whom had been educated in colleges and seminaries colored by the liberal theology of the thirties. They had all been members of meditation groups at various times and had a common practice of silent prayer. The purpose of their relationship was to discover ways to give meaning and power to their daily living. During the first months each of the ten members gave in a deliberate manner his spiritual autobiography. When this had been done, it became evident that each had gone through the painful experience of discovering the inadequacy of his liberal faith to meet the exigencies of the world in which he lived. The Kingdom of God could not be established, the members were convinced, by radical social ethics. Their discovery turned them to an examination of their spiritual tools: what did each one actually believe about God, Christ, sin, grace, love, atonement, forgiveness? These were looked at through life's experiences instead of being clothed with traditional, intellectual terms with which all were more or less familiar. By deep, intimate and honest inquiry the cell members have found ways to help one another to the Source of love and joy and peace.

This group begins its meetings with a forty-five-minute period of silence as described in the preceding chapter. The silence is broken by a person who serves as co-ordinator. A simple meal is served, the women in the group rotating alphabetically in making soup. The conversation at the table is a free exchange of mutual activities. The after-supper sharing as described herein always has precedence, unless someone has an urgent need with which group members are asked to help. One principle safeguards this group from becoming a discussion club. The search is for Spiritual Truth and an application of this truth to life. No speech-making, argumentation, or pooling of mere information is in order here.

SHARING PROBLEMS

Sharing faith in fundamental truths but holds a mirror before the participants so that they behold their weaknesses and failures. This, too, is healthy in a closely-knit group where all are seekers who have confidence in one another. In the beginning such periods may be superficial and even embarrassing to all involved, but a genuine desire for truth is bound to open up the basic difficulties.

One teacher, for instance, came to his prayer fellowship, without his usual bubbling good nature. He was frankly discouraged and appeared quite defeated. His problem was that of a Christian, working in a materialistic, openly anti-Christian situation, who, aspiring "to carry all before him" by his newly-found faith, suddenly became aware that he was not popular. The whole matter had come to the forefront when a fellow teacher attacked him in public. As he told the story, certain elements emerged which both he and his fellows saw simultaneously. An undercurrent of fear was operating beneath his usual joyous exterior that affected his relationships and unbalanced his actions. When he recognized this fact in the mirror of his friends' concern, he gradually came to have new freedom and strength. But before the fellowship had worked through this man's difficulty, the other members discovered the same current of fear in themselves. In the free give-and-take of a concerned and honest judgment, such revelations come so that all are enabled to walk on with greater courage than they ever knew before.

Sharing Sins

John Woolman often referred to the communion of sin. No man lives alone: by goodness all are lifted heavenward and by evil all are given a backward thrust. Vicarious suffering becomes sooner or later the portion of a deeply sharing prayer group for "no man is an island."

One source of loneliness or cut-offness is a sense of guilt. Sinners are inevitable wall constructionists. They use most of their energy in keeping their walls in repair and making them impenetrable. They dare not be spontaneous. In the warmth of a loving cell the partitions begin to break down. There comes about an unpremeditated confession. When this occurs, there must always be kept before the group the fact that their chief concern is to find God's answer to the problem and that they are never to fasten onto the problem itself. A public confession of weakness or overt sin is always painful for all concerned, but if it is a sincere pouring-out of one's heart before those who love and manifest a loving concern and judgment, it can "work together for good." One rule given by an experienced pastoral counselor has point here: "Once a sin is confessed and forgiveness experienced, there must under no circumstances be any digging up."

The act of confession is usually better performed in the presence of a minister or counselor than in the prayer group. Yet if it is made in such a meeting and properly received, it may become the means of transforming the lonely sinner into the lovely man or woman that God intended. In such an experience, each person is challenged to be honest, and each discovers beneath the overt act the root of good or evil to be nurtured or destroyed, as the case may be. All engage with renewed determination to help one another. They say something like this: "Let us be good altogether! Let us know that the *real* part of each of us is the best part, the believing part, the loving part."

"The final grounds of Holy Fellowship are in God. Lives immersed and drowned in God are drowned in love, and know one another in Him, and know one another in love. God is the medium, the matrix, the focus, the solvent. . . . Such lives have a common meeting point. . . . Persons in the Fellowship are related to one another in Him, as all mountains go down to the same earth."[1]

[1] Thomas Kelly, *op. cit.*, p. 83.

VI

The Intercessory Group

When we come to prayer [says Gerald Heard], we must take people who are with us. We can't leave them outside. . . . God gave you the company of fellow-seekers—the company of the holy. We must keep together! The bees cannot make their wax (all their honey goes to waste) unless they can come together, perfectly still, out of their incessantly active life. When the wax begins to form under the wings, they can build these cells which will hold the honey. We must meet together. Never forget that, the company of the holy. We must keep together.

Tennyson's line: "For so the whole round earth is every way bound by gold chains about the feet of God!" Yes! bound to Him, but also bound to one another! And if we are not doing that, we are not taking the benefits which we were meant to have and we are not giving them, either. We help others, and they help us. We cannot be saved without others.[1]

In this sense every prayer cell is an intercessory prayer cell. Members of the meditation group and sharing group cannot escape praying in behalf of their comrades of the spirit. Bound together by a unique tie, each inevitably becomes involved in the crises of every other member. To love means to make intercession. By this kind of prayer we do not mean holding pleasant thoughts about people—intercession requires bringing our own wills into harmony with God plus a sustained effort in behalf of those for whom we pray. For instance, someone is going through a great temptation. The situation is almost overwhelming and apparently hopeless. Those who pray must seek to understand the circumstances and try to see the will of God; then offer themselves and all they have to God in the

[1] Gerald Heard: *Ten Questions on Prayer*. Pendle Hill pamphlet, Wallingford, Pennsylvania, 1951, pp. 3 and 32.

interest of that person. Such a prayer of good will alters the situation, and too, it may reveal a course of action to those who are praying. The same may be said for prayers for peace and for other "cause" prayers.

This chapter, however, is concerned with companies of people who come together regularly and primarily to make intercession. Such groups usually are intiated because of a specific need: someone may be sick, physically or mentally; someone may be lonely; some public catastrophe may have brought a group into existence. The dire need for world peace may bring about prayer vigils, prayer chains. Prayer for peace has brought more people together than any other form of corporate prayer.

"There is no principle of the heart that is more acceptable to God," says William Law, "than an universal fervent love to all mankind, wishing and praying for their happiness; because there is no principle of the heart that makes us more like God, who is love and goodness itself, and created all beings for their enjoyment of happiness." [2] Since it is the natural impulse of the heart to pray for others, it is no wonder that this form of prayer cell leads all the others.

Conceptions of intercessory prayer vary considerably. There are points, however, at which most agree. Intercessory prayer does not presume to change the course of God's good will, nor to exercise a superior power over another's life. This form of prayer assumes that the love of God is already at work in the situation, and prayer, if it is true prayer, is co-operation with God's own love. For those praying become channels of His healing energy. As a person selflessly submits himself to Divine direction he becomes increasingly sensitive to the will of God for the person for whom he prays. So it is that an eminent spiritual healer is sustained by a group of people in her home church and she turns to them often for guidance when asked to intercede for the healing of the sick.

Another facet of intercessory prayer commonly accepted is that it is a means by which scattered forces for good are brought into focus so that persons and movements are linked to spiritual power.

[2] William Law: A Serious Call to a Devout and Holy Life (Philadelphia: Westminster Press, 1948), p. 278.

Not only is the subject of such prayer renewed but he who prays also is often revitalized. As mentioned earlier, persons have come to their cell tired and unalive, and have gone away from the corporate prayer for others with a quiet strength and inflow of power that made them radiant. God is like a good gardener who repairs the implement when He uses it. Catherine of Siena stands as the classic example of the renewing power of intercessory prayer. She discovered that when her interior prayer was dry, if she held others in the light of God, her own heart was warmed and her spirit took fire. This is the miracle—when an individual offers his weaknesses and incapacities for another person, he is blessed by God. To the level of intensity that the will is turned in love to God one calls forth that love for others.

When we pray together we multiply our strength. As the good Rabbi Mikhail puts it, "I join myself to all of Israel, to those who are more than I, that through them my thought may rise and to those who are less than I so that they may rise through my prayer."

The patterns used by groups vary. Most groups carry on without any rigid order. A woman's group follows this simple pattern: They meet in one another's homes, the hostess serving as the co-ordinator. When there is a record player available, the meeting begins and closes with worshipful music, the music setting the tone of the hour together. "O Rest in the Lord," "Jesu, Joy of Man's Desiring," "The Lord's Prayer," carry the group members directly into the purpose of their gathering. Hymn singing serves the same purpose, "Jesus Stand Among Us" being a favorite. The leader conducts a simple meditation, reading perhaps from Scriptures. A period of silence, generally brief, follows, so that the meaning of the reading sinks into the minds of all. The hostess breaks the silence by expressing those concerns that she finds most urgent. She makes no effort to be comprehensive because it is the practice of this cell to refrain from repetition.

Some groups invite repetition as being helpful. In the fellowship of which we are writing, however, each person prays silently as the hostess presents those concerns for which she thinks the group should pray. When the leader has finished her list, the friend to her left carries on; and so on around the circle. There is no hurry and there are frequent silences. Sometimes the rotation is abandoned and members pray as they are led. The hostess may then close the meeting with a prayer and a corporate offering of the Lord's Prayer.

One leader of an intercessory prayer group begins every session by stating the two essentials of prayer for others: faith, and a determined will to goodness for him who is prayed for. To care for the subject of the prayer is necessary. She then states two facts about prayer: Prayer is eternal, extending beyond the mere words in which it is couched; it goes on working forever in the subconsciousness of him who utters it and affects the whole atmosphere. In intercessory prayer God permits His creature to co-operate in the work of creation. God is an eternal will to goodness and when anyone turns himself to willing goodness for others God uses him as a vessel.

A recollection of these two facts gives to those about to engage in the work of intercession a sense of the dignity and responsibility involved in it.

Whatever the context of the prayer, whether it is "holding another in the Light," or envisioning him in the center of God's never-failing stream of love, joy and peace, the person praying begins by placing himself in relationship to God. The leader of such a group writes:

First, we remind ourselves of His compassion, His joy, His peace. Bathed in that unending river of goodness we draw with us those who are most precious to us. We recognize our weaknesses and sins but we rejoice that if we hold firmly on to God we strengthen those we love.

At this point we pause and in silence, or vocal prayer, each one prays for his family and friends. As the needs of friends are mentioned the group makes intercession for them corporately. It is amazing how naturally we all are concerned for the friends of our friends. The sympathy and love of one member opens the door to the sympathy and concern of another.

Our next step is to pray for those who make us unhappy. We take literally the scripture "Pray for your enemies and those who despitefully use you." We believe that we are bound by hatred and that freedom is found in its transformation into right relationship. It has been our experience that when we gather our so-called enemies into the Presence of God, we discover our own inadequacies as well. By praying together about our enemies we have definitely closed some distressing gaps in the human family.

The fourth part of our prayer hour is given to prayer for special needs —locally, in the Church, nationally, and for the peace of the world. Sometimes these needs demand most of our time together. We are led by a sense of what is most important at the time.

We may use many symbols to keep ourselves centered, such as "the stream of God's love." Another symbol we use is that of "the clasped hand" or the "foot of the Cross where the love of God became manifest to the human family." As one seeks to clasp the hand of the Divine, he yearns for that connection to become real for his fellow creatures, both friend and foe. Out of such a season of prayer we are led to extend our hands both spiritually and actually to those about us.

Another form helpful to us is the use of a hymn as the carrier of the intercession. For instance, the following words have become for us a prayer for peace between individuals and in the world. We use it many times when we are at work in our homes and in our private devotions:

> "O God of peace,
> Who healest the broken lives of the world
> Unite us we pray thee.
>
> O God of peace,
> Who healest the wounds mankind gives to man,
> Unite us we pray thee.
>
> O God of peace,
> Who willest all life to enter Thy peace
> Unite us in thee."

Many prayer groups make use of the Book of Common Prayer and other orders of worship. Some Third Order groups have a formalized ritual that is observed by the members not only when they come together but as they go about their daily lives. One group has made use of a less formal intercession based on a prayer from the East:

> O God, Thou art Peace.
> We are surrounded by Thy peace.
> We are filled with Thy peace.
> Thy Peace is above us,
>   beneath us,
>   within us.

Such Peace is ours.
And all is well.

May Thy Peace be to all beings,
May it be between all beings,
And may it come from all beings.

The leader recites the first part as a prayer and then in silence all the members let themselves be caught up into the spirit of God's peace. The leader then with short prayers directs the attention of the group first toward one direction of the earth and then proceeds out in ever larger concentric circles (*e.g.,* O God, may Thy peace be with all people in the United States to the East of us. Then to the islands of the Atlantic, and then the countries of Europe and the Near East). The same procedure is then followed toward the other three directions. When an area of special concern is reached a longer time is spent and the leader includes that special need in his prayer. In the intervening silences others in the group pray in harmony with the prayer of the leader.

This prayer period is opened and closed by a hymn of peace:

May Thy peace which is extending,
Father who embraces all,
Past all depth of our misgiving,
Past all height of understanding,
Keep our every thought and feeling
In Thy knowledge and Thy love.

One thing an intercessory prayer cell cannot do with impunity is to "look back over its shoulder" after a prayer experience to see how God is working it out. God perhaps keeps us from seeing the results of the prayer He has worked through us, because as Gerald Heard suggests, "He knows we would say, 'I did that! I helped that person with my prayers!'" The end is out of sight. Our only duty is to sustain one another.

A many-colored bird nested in the top branches of a very tall tree in a far-off birdless land. The people who had but glimpsed such a treasure longed for it. To possess it the men made of themselves a living ladder, standing on one another's shoulders until they almost reached the top. Those who were the highest could see the rare beauty almost within their reach. Those who stood nearest the ground could not see it and they grew weary of holding their brothers. They gave up, shook themselves free and the ladder collapsed, though with a little patience that for which they all sought would soon have been revealed. We are so impatient when we do not see, and in our ignorance fail not only ourselves but all those depending upon us. Our prayers at best are far from perfect. Nevertheless, we must indeed leave all results to God, asking that His will be done, and believing that in His power we will hold fast. For always "the Spirit helps us in our weakness; for we do not know how to pray as we ought, but the Spirit himself intercedes for us" (Romans 8:26, r.s.v.).

VII

Workout and Study Groups

THE WORKOUT GROUP

One cannot honestly pray without living a life of sacrificial action because a willingness to give oneself for others is a corollary of prayer. Sometimes the criticism is made that persons join prayer cells to avoid the responsibilities expected of church members. Not so frequent but none the less regrettable is the criticism that many church members plunge into a round of activities to escape the spiritual implications of church membership. "But there is no hidin' place down there," as the spiritual says.

God made us to breathe in and then out. As Francis of Sales says, affective (the in-breathing) love and effective (the out-breathing) love are but two facets of the same love. We cannot live spiritually or physically without both, nor can a cell. A group that meets together simply to strengthen its members soon becomes ingrown and unhealthily introspective. An excellent antidote is to have a periodical workout—a time when the members can get together on a down-to-earth job. Particularly is this true if they are not working on some phase of a Christian service program. Many times individuals will find a challenging work project, but there are other times when it is highly desirable for the group to work together.

It matters little what the actual projects are, just so the experience of fellowship finds release in creative service for others. The president of a woman's society in a church hesitated about joining a prayer cell. Several months later she sought membership. "I'll tell you why," she said to her minister. "Last fall I asked several folk entering the cell to serve on committees of the woman's society, and they refused. Later I asked them again, and this time I didn't get a refusal! I want to be a member of a cell that does that to people!"

Out of a growing understanding of Christian service that such a simple illustration reveals comes the helpfulness that is fellowship in action. Folks who begin by sharing the task of a program committee in a local church society end up by accepting larger tasks to meet their growing spirits.

There are, of course, cells whose purpose is the accomplishment of particular work in church or community. For instance, one woman was chairman of the committee to select a minister for a small community church. She was very much interested in prayer cells and led the committee members into forming a prayer cell as they proceeded to find a pastor.

Another active woman's committee discovered the value of preceding their work by a period of prayer at the church altar. This practice has continued throughout the years. Another workout cell is made up of youth leaders in a large city. They felt the necessity of bringing to their respective churches prayer groups for young people. They met together weekly for thirty minutes of prayer, and then spent an equal amount of time in study and pooling of plans to carry out their purposes.

The following description of a workout cell is given in the words of John H. Ryder, a businessman who brought prayer into his office.

I was trying to study the Bible and pray every night at home. My prayer time became the most important part of my day and I saw that it should start every morning. Above all, it should be a set time with no interruptions! Actually my office proved to be the best place for this; so while I continued to pray at night, I began to set aside thirty minutes or more at my desk every morning, before regular business hours. Although everyone was welcome to join me, only Bill came at first. For months we two studied and prayed together. Gradually, others, *seeing the change in us,* asked if they could come.

Looking back, I can see that God was forming a team—and because of those He brought, we have more and more been able as a group to seek His help in policy matters and other major business problems. God wants to use different ones in different ways. I know there are not a few groups made up of top executives and the men who control the company, and also others composed of those in a certain department, or from the rank and file.

Usually we have at least six who attend every morning. These six include our department heads. Most of our sales managers take part whenever they are in town. A dozen or more of our men travelling all over this country and Canada also pray with us at this same hour, or during their own regular prayer times.

From the very beginning, we have followed a simple pattern: we usually discuss our problems the day before; then sleep on them. The next morning we start our day in prayer, offering up these problems to God. Each day leadership rotates to a different member of the team who opens by reading a chapter from the New Testament. Next this leader may pray extemporaneously and then he leads us in the Lord's Prayer.

In the period of silence we then offer up ourselves and our problems to God and *listen* for His answer. We always write down any thoughts and directions that come to us, and towards the end of our time together the leader asks each one to read whatever he has written. If a specific problem is still unanswered, or if we are in disagreement about it, we never act on it. We offer it up during the day in individual prayer and at the next meeting, until God's answer becomes clear. I do not order my executives to do anything. We either act in love and unison, or not at all. Each meeting concludes with intercessory prayers for anyone who requests them.[1]

In a similar manner prayer groups have concerned themselves with the great problems of war and peace, with the persistent problems of race relations, with the undergirding and guiding of a venture in religious publication. Conceivably, every activity or organization that is under the direction of religious people could be conducted with the staff serving as a spiritual team in a workout prayer group. Many churches might well profit by adapting these principles to the conduct of their corporate life in the service of God and man.

THE STUDY GROUP

As we have discussed these various types of cells in some detail, it has become evident that each of them is a study group. There are

[1] *The Evangel*, January-February, 1953.

innumerable study groups in the religious life of the Church. It is not for lack of education that we are spiritually undeveloped. A study group becomes a prayer cell when its primary purpose is to gain skill in Christian living. In other words, a study group becomes a prayer group when the study is a springboard for meditation and sharing.

Many times a sharing cell may wear itself out and the meeting hour may drift into futile pooling of group ignorance. Then it is time to choose a study that goes deeper than any that the members have yet ventured to undertake. The aim of such exploration is to learn principles, to discover ways of applying those principles to daily practice, and to recover inspiration to make daily life more radiant.

Most men and women are ill at ease in prayer. Their lives are so crowded that there is little chance that their desire to pray will crystallize into a habit. It is therefore good for persons with even a faint desire to know how to pray to get together for the sole purpose of learning this art. A few "primers of prayer" are available. Jesus conducted a School of Prayer when his disciples asked for it. A study group not only informs us but it also becomes in a way a strong defense against skeptical friends.

One meditation group prepared for itself a course of study from various spiritual classics, based on the expressed needs of its members. The Bible, of course, is the chief sourcebook of study. Many groups come together to study the Bible, and develop into one of the four kinds of cells already mentioned. The following account is of a cell that for two years has been working through the Gospel of Matthew.

Early in their study together the members decided that of the three possible approaches to Scripture (1) an acceptance of each verse as being inspired and historically true; (2) an acceptance of the findings of higher criticism and a dissecting of Scripture verse by verse to determine authentic and unauthentic passages; and (3) a reading of Scripture to discover the timeless truths therein and to apply them to one's own spiritual development, the third method was the way that opened up life. As one member put it, this meant "finding the Truth written in one's soul." The real Truth lies back of the parable, of course, whether the interpretation takes the form of a historic judgment, an individual judgment or an inner judgment.

This study group has met once a week during the two years with only a few interruptions. Each member uses one of the various accepted translations. A passage in a chapter is read—it may be a verse or a paragraph or a full section—and the various translations are compared. Then there follows a short period of silence during which the seekers center themselves on the verses. As they consider an outward event, it becomes the inner event of the soul. Here is a summary of the session devoted to Jesus' parable of the sheep and the goats at the Last Judgment (Matthew 25:31–46). The parable might be interpreted, it was mentioned, as a foreshadowing of the events of history and the truth in no way diminished! It may be a judgment of people. Or it may be a picture of the good and evil forces within the human soul, the interpretation dwelt on by this group. The day of judgment becomes the condemnation of the Indwelling Christ. The sheep are the sacrifice, the human will given over to the Divine will; the goats are the undisciplined wanderers, devouring the will. These two natures are inherent in each person. The test of the salvation of the sheep seems at first glance to be love or ministry to need. Upon further investigation it develops that salvation comes because of awareness of life and its need, acceptance of the hungry, the imprisoned, and the naked, and a spontaneous giving to them. The goats were not even aware of the needy, so engrossed were they in their own superficial affairs. The key is in discerning and being sensitive to need, to which one can minister in compassion. Every person and every need is included as a being or a matter to be given loving concern. Exclusive goats wandered willfully about their own concerns, cut off from the fullness of life. Inclusive sheep centered intently on the deep needs of the human soul—their own and others'—and found life eternal.

This story, worked out bit by bit, stirred the group members in the silent period that followed to a renewed resolution to die to self and to live to God.

Such a study of Scripture is not easy for persons to whom the

Bible is very familiar. To read Bible passages with which one has grown up as if they are being heard for the first time can come about only if one can voluntarily set aside old interpretations and yield to the Spirit. To approach them, however, with the simplicity of a little child clothes them with inspiration and with life. Once one has quit temporizing and stops saying, "Now did Jesus really say this? Or did Matthew put it down to conform with some ideas of his own?" and approaches the passage positively in the spirit of "Here is truth for me in my spiritual need—Lord, open thou mine eyes," then there comes the brightness, warmth and enthusiasm of a new experience. New revelations of God's will and wisdom sparkle through the well-known words. The mind that so inquires never grows old. As it was said of an ancient Friend, "She was ninety-four and her mind was alert and growing." Some psychologists are saying that if the intellectual powers are not allowed to become "stiff at the joints" in the middle years, the maturing process is continued and the wisdom of old age is an actuality.

PREPARING MEDITATIONS AND HELPS

In Part Two will be found meditations and papers for use in prayer cells over a period of thirty weeks. These were prepared for specific groups that met from October into May, meeting each week except during the holiday season. Groups in other churches have used them and have found them helpful.

But they are not to be slavishly followed. Even though they grew week by week out of the struggling needs of one church, and gave nourishment to all concerned, they are frankly the expression of the personality of one man and one church. Still, they give insight into the way a beginning leader and group may start the long, hard trail to the Delectable Mountains.

For those with even the slightest flair of creative ability, it will be a deep joy to prepare one's own set of meditations. These can be used as the directed meditations for a prayer cell, or for services of worship where there is directed prayer or meditation through silence, or for one's own private devotional use. They capture a thought that can be jotted down in brief, and later expanded into a meditation not only for temporary reading but also for permanent recording.

These suggestions will help in the creating of such meditations. First, choose a single theme, treating it from one or more points of view, but making sure that no extraneous material is brought in. Let it be a large theme if you wish, such as "The Love of God," but make sure that it considers only one phase of that theme, God's love for me, God's love revealed through someone, God's love so freely given. Too many thoughts create a wandering mind, and a meditation should center on one idea, driving it home.

Second, be brief. Approximately 200-250 words, about what will take a half page when typewritten single-spaced, is a good measure for completing a theme. If more words are needed, the theme is normally too large and should be broken down into smaller ones.

Third, always write in the first person singular. If "we" is used, the reader thinks of a group, and is not so conscious of his own relationship to the theme. If "you" is used, the reader thinks only of others, not of himself. "I" and "me" are not self-centering words always; they merely say that this reading concerns *me*, the reader.

Fourth, let examination of self always be a part of the meditation, so that if questions are not directly asked, at least they are implied. What is my relationship to the theme? Is the question basic to preparing a meditation? How does it affect me? What must I do about it? Where have I failed or where have I succeeded?

Fifth, the examination of self may be negative in the early part, but the closing part should always be positive. The first part may point out my weakness, my inadequacy, my helplessness, my wrong-doing, and these we must see if we are to grow. But the second part should point toward God's strength and helpfulness and goodness and love and mercy by which my weakness is made strong, my imperfection made perfect, my uselessness made usefulness.

Sixth, direct the words mostly to God, like a prayer. Do not speak indirectly to God as *He will*, but directly as *Thou wilt*; I forget *Thee* (not Him), I would serve *Thee* (not Him or His Spirit).

Seventh, let the imagination have a free rein beforehand, until it fastens upon a single theme; then control it in the growth of that single theme. Feed the imagination by long hours of reading, of the Bible in general and the Psalms in particular and the Gospels especially, and of devotional books and pamphlets that reveal the search of others and their finding. Whenever a thought comes to mind, jot it down at the time, so that later it may be developed into a full-length meditation. Otherwise, the seed that God has planted is blown away by the winds of our forgetting.

So much for suggestions as to preparing directed meditations. To prepare the papers of exercises and instructions and helps to be taken home each week by members of the cell groups is quite different. These will vary greatly according to the theme, but one thing must be emphasized over and over again: let simplicity of words and thought be paramount. If it seems wise at the moment to lean toward long, involved words or cloudy theological phrases, WAIT! Search most diligently for simpler words and phrases. It is better to have someone say with surprise: "Why! I understood every word of it!" than to have one say: "It must be brilliant writing, for it was all over my head."

The papers used in Part Two evolved over a long period of time, in recognition of the spiritual progression revealed almost identically in several differing cells. First comes the clear direction as to what we are to do, and the foundations upon which we are to build our spiritual growth. Then come specific exercises, for cells are primarily schools for the practice of prayer, not for the study of prayer (though such study of prayer will be "extracurricular" activity for many cell members).

Next will come papers suggesting the use of silence, of intercessory prayer, of other methods that help in prayer, plus hints from time to time on certain fundamental principles, such as an understanding of spiritual dryness, almost universal in about the seventh or eighth week. This alternation continues, of exercise and fundamentals, as the progression moves along.

PART TWO

Meditations and Helps

INTRODUCTION

The success of the first meeting of such prayer groups as are described in this second part is intrinsic to their success as groups. Hence, we are giving the pattern used in full detail.

The minister or layman who extends the invitation to his congregation to become members of a prayer fellowship explains to each person the nature of the studies to be pursued together. The method of conducting the hour is clearly set forth. What one will do upon arrival, what will happen there, how each may share, are suggested, with the understanding, of course, that the group itself will have the final say on what happens, according to the growth of the members. Thus, no one comes to the first meeting without understanding a little of the procedure, even though what may happen to the person involved rests in the hands of God.

Second, the preparation necessary before coming into the group is explained. Each person is told exactly where the cell will meet, and exactly at what hour. Promptness is emphasized. Everyone who comes will discover on a table, readily seen, the printed meditations which he is to take into the meeting room. These are to be read and then reread, until a thought or phrase catches the mind. He lets this thought wander over and over again through his mind until it speaks clearly to his inner mind. These are the words to be shared in a later period. Everyone is asked to bring his Bible or other devotional reading. This will be used for the remainder of the time of silence that is left after the reading of the directed meditation, its study and its putting aside.

Since some of the prayer group will not know how to pray, they should be told that after sitting down quietly they should pray the words of the Lord's Prayer, saying each word slowly. In the first meeting they will receive suggestions how next to pray.

Third, before anyone comes, the discipline which each member is to accept is thoroughly explained. It is in three minimum parts. First, all agree to attend regularly for a stated period of time. In one church all agree to attend from the first of October to Christmas. If it is suggested that they must attend an entire year, it frightens some. Nearly all will agree to three months (less time will be too short for true growth of spirit), and most will then want to continue beyond the short term. Second, each person agrees to pray each day in his own quiet time (hour and place and length of period to be one's own choice) by name for each other person in his group. Announce that this will be explained in the first meeting, so that learners in prayer will know what to say. Third, each person agrees to pray each day for the minister and congregation as they meet together on the Sunday next. This threefold simple minimum discipline is the first step in creating a true fellowship, really basic to all else.

Fourth, as to the first meeting. It will be divided into two parts of thirty minutes each: first, a time of silence; second, a time of sharing. The leader will have prepared the room, placing the directed meditations upon a table. A collection of devotional books and various translations of the Bible will be available. People coming to the cell will take up a meditation, and enter quietly into the meeting room, carrying along with them their other devotional readings. (Often folk wish to take notes, but forget to carry pencils. Have a few on the table with the meditations.) They will be seated either in alternate chairs or in chairs placed far enough apart to avoid a sense of crowding. Handbags, Bibles and the like should be placed carefully on the alternate chairs or on the floor, freeing one from the distractions of falling things.

In the time of silence each will read his meditation, search for a thought for himself, continue with other reading, and offer what prayers he may wish. It is silence, not stillness of body, that is the rule. Quiet in time takes hold of our spirits and all is quiet. With growth of spirit through the weeks and months that silence becomes truly Creative Silence.

At the end of thirty minutes of silence, the leader will break it with requests for intercession as they may arise. These will usually be for sick folk at first, though many other requests will come after the cell gets into its true movement. Each request will be followed by a moment of silence in which the members will offer their own prayer in line with the request. Then the group will join in a slow and careful praying of the Lord's Prayer.

Now begins the second part, the sharing. The leader should mention his insight or question as it came to him from his reading of the directed meditation. Though many questions and comments will arise after this first one by the leader, most of them, because all have used the same meditation, will usually center around that single theme. Between comments there may be periods of silence. These are never to be feared, even when they become quite long. Nor should the leader force the sharing by making additional comment, though at times he may wish to do so.

Just before the close of the hour, the leader will present the paper for that week, calling attention to the exercises to be practiced during the week, or to the instructions as to prayer for others as agreed to in the discipline. Then any questions as to procedure should be carefully answered. The session is brought to a close by a benediction, many groups using corporately the Mizpah benediction ("The Lord watch between me and thee, while we are absent, one from the other").

Fifth, as to further reading of devotional books. Some churches have gathered together copies of spiritual classics. The book table wherever available always becomes one of the most valuable adjuncts of the cell group. In one church thirty to forty books are in constant circulation every week. The leader needs wisdom in recommending to the members of the cell group those books most helpful for their condition. In time, members themselves will tell others of classics that did feed their spirits. The annotated bibliography in Appendix I will be valuable at this point.

The second meeting is like the first, except in the time of sharing. Near the end of that period, inquiry will be made by the leader as to the practice of the quiet time during the week (the exercise of the first paper). So each week inquiry will be made concerning the paper presented the week before. Then just before the benediction, the new paper for the week ahead is passed out.

(For those prayer groups that use these meditations and helps as presented in this Part Two, a copy of the book itself will be taken into the meeting room by each member. The meditation for the week assigned will be read carefully, and then the paper for the ensuing days will be read each day at home as the cell member practices the exercises or studies the fundamentals. For an individual unable to find a group, this material may be used in the same way; the weekly aids to be followed intensively, rather than a reading of the entire series at one sitting.)

1

The First Week

THE MEDITATION

My name is Legion. I am many persons, instead of one person.

I am Suspicion, sensitive to slights imagined or real, afraid someone is talking about me.

I am Resentment, not liking certain folk, afraid they are trying to put something over on me, trying to take advantage of me.

I am Envy, unable to understand why some people have what I want but don't have.

I am Anger, flaring up at the slightest irritation.

I am Bitterness, complaining at my lot in life, kicking against circumstance.

I am Fear, afraid to try something new, lest I fail; afraid to accept responsibility, lest I can't carry on.

I am Contempt, scorning those who can't move as fast as I do, think as quickly as I do, pray as easily as I do, give as liberally as I do.

I am Greed, holding back for myself more than I need, excusing my stinginess by my small income.

I am Pride, sure of my place, condescending to those "less fortunate."

I am Self, thinking of self, dreaming of self, desiring for self, loving self.

I want to be one person, a person with a Center. I believe that I can be whole. With trust and in love I give my many selves to Thee. Take what I have this moment, of weakness and strength, of confusion and assurance, of doubt and faith, of dark moods and joyous radiance. All that I have I place in Your hands. Here is my Life.

Now that I turn my back upon myself, and look toward Thee, through me bless my home, my church, my community. Thou art my Joy, my Peace, my Strength. With these my friends in this Fellowship may I take day by day each day as it comes, knowing that Thou art with me, that Thou dost speak to me in the silence, that Thou dost lead me.

The Paper

WE BEGIN OUR EXPERIMENTS

We come together in fellowship once a week to learn how to grow spiritually into the fullness of the Christian life. It is a slow process, demanding persistence and patience. Frequently we will be tempted to say, "What's the use? I don't seem to be growing better. I may even be growing worse! Really, nothing is happening to me."

The truth is, some of us will notice an inward change very quickly, which will not be recognizable to others for some time. Others of us will wonder if anything is going to happen, only to find quite suddenly that something HAS. God will come into our lives as soon as we are ready for Him.

To help prepare ourselves for His coming, two things are necessary. First, we must yield ourselves to him. Prayer, after all, is yielding. We must say, from head and heart: "Here am I, take me." Hour after hour through the days and nights we must continually offer ourselves by saying within: "I place myself in Thy hands. I want to follow Thy leadership. Teach me to listen to Thy voice in every moment of the day. No matter what happens to me I know that Thou art with me. I am not alone."

Basic to all we do together is this prayer of yielding. We must return to it time and time again, until we live it without thinking about it, a habit that becomes fixed by repetition.

Second is the discipline of daily practice of the quiet time. If this is not most faithfully followed, little will happen that is good for us. But when it is most faithfully followed, strange and wondrous things will happen. We do not follow a set hour or an agreed length of time for our quiet period. It is best that it be as early in the morning as possible, but it may have to be in the evening. It should start with no less than five minutes, and gradually it ought to grow into a minimum of fifteen minutes, then longer as we can make the time.

In this quiet time we will read the Bible or devotional books, practice our various exercises, pray, and learn to sit in listening quiet that God may speak. We follow no prescribed plan or program, each one developing that which seems best to him through experience. But we do agree to a twofold discipline.

One, each one of us each day will pray for each other person in our group.

At first these will be very brief prayers until we become acquainted. They may be such as this one: "Bless Thou A—— whom I hold before Thee in love. Let Thy spirit of quiet rest upon her." Later, we will add to the prayer as we learn that on one day our friend will be facing a new task or a difficult problem or has received some special blessing.

Two, each one of us each day will pray for the minister and the congregation as they come together on the following Sunday, that God's blessing may rest upon the worship, that His presence may be revealed in words said and sung and in prayer expressed or unexpressed.

Other than these two simple prayers, as a group we do not assume a discipline. Many of us will share in other requests for prayer from time to time; but these two are the ones basic to our fellowship.

Begin immediately this daily practice, and be ready in our next session to report on the finding of time, the length of the period, and the use of this quiet hour.

2

The Second Week

THE MEDITATION

Thanks be unto Thee, O God, for Thy hand upon my life. Thou
hast placed me in the midst of a family where I can know something of the fullness of life. Thou hast given me friends whose love
and affection bring me warmth and good cheer. Thou hast given
me work to do in which I may find creative joy. Thou hast given
me leisure in which to play and read and think, building things
of the spiritual world to stand side by side with the things of
the material world.

Thou art far off, a God hidden from my eyes and from my ears;
yet Thou art very near, speaking to me in the silence of my better
thoughts, revealing Thyself to me through my inner eye. Early in
the morning Thou art with me, and in the night hours Thou
dost watch over me. Thy love for me is too great for me, for I am
not worthy of it. Still, Thou dost pour out upon me like waters
from the heavens the fullness of Thy Spirit.

O my soul, rejoice in the blessings that come to you from the
hand of the Living God. My God is a great God, whose spirit
moves me to lift up my eyes to His beauty, to His truth, to His
goodness. Thou art Love, O Thou Eternal One, and in Thy love
I find the depths of my joy.

THE PAPER

FOUNDATIONS OF CHRISTIAN PRAYER

We are just beginning a systematic practice of prayer and the
devotional life. We have learned that our basic attitude must be
the yielding of ourselves without any reservation. "Here am I,
take me" is to be the key sentence of our lives.

But to Whom do we yield ourselves? To what kind of God are we offering ourselves? This makes all the difference in the world. Before a God of fear or vengeance we would come with fear and much appeasement. Before a God of caprice we would come with carefully laid plans to win Him to our thinking and desire.

As Christians we yield ourselves to the God of Jesus Christ, the Father of each one of us, who combines His justice and His mercy in love. It is Douglas Steere who suggests there are three presuppositions to Christian prayer, which are the foundations for all our seeking. Let us consider each one thoughtfully this week.

First, God is seeking us, He Himself taking the initiative. We do not turn first to Him. He has already started drawing us to Himself. Patiently He has been waiting until we would turn to Him, and during His waiting, He has given us experience after experience in which He has been revealing Himself. Suddenly we recognize His hand, and follow His beckoning. So it is that some of us have come into these groups not so much by our own choice as by the suggestions of daily life through friends or incidents that suddenly have made us aware of God's calling. Charles Whiston in *Teach Us to Pray*, calls the initiative of God His "prevenience." "Long before we begin to pray at all," he writes, "God has already been acting in and upon us, preparing the way for our response." [1] (See Chapter 2 of that fine book.) So it was that John wrote so long ago: "We love him, because he first loved us" (I John 4:19). We can pray to Him and listen to Him because He is always ready, there first, waiting for us.

Second, God cares infinitely for us, loving us as His children. He has blessed us all out of proportion to what we deserve or merit. We cannot come to Him and demand a single thing, expecting it will be handed to us, JUST BECAUSE we are good, or will be good. Out of the bounty of His own gracious love, He gives us what we need and far more, merely through asking in the name and spirit of Jesus. Our sorrow is relieved by His sorrow, our joy is brightened by His joy, our longing is answered by His longing.

[1] Charles Whiston: *Teach Us to Pray* (Boston: The Pilgrim Press, 1949) p. 21.

Again it was John who wrote: "If we confess our sins, he is faithful and just to forgive us our sins, and to cleanse us from all unrighteousness" (I John 1:9). With great love He watches over us every moment of the day and night.

Third, God still is revealing Himself to us. Even today through the Bible and other devotional books, through the wonders of nature, through the friendship of comrades, through the strange workings of daily experience He speaks to us. We can know His will for us today. Sometimes it is with judgment, sometimes with love, sometimes with warning; yet, in many ways God even in our day reveals Himself to each one of us. That is what Jesus meant when He said: "But the Comforter, which is the Holy Ghost, whom the Father will send in my name, he shall teach you all things" (John 14:26a). Each one of us, before this week has gone, can expect God's revelation of Himself to our own inner life, a revelation certain and sure.

As we continue our twofold discipline in our quiet time, and as we begin to add to our prayers for ourselves and for others, let us examine these three foundations of our prayer, seeing where He is seeking us, does love us, still continues to reveal Himself. Then let us share next week what we have discovered.

3

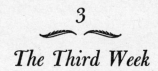

The Third Week

THE MEDITATION

I stand in need before Thee. I want to get, and not give. I seek a peace of mind and heart that will be a pleasant path for me to walk upon, where the birds sing and the flowers bloom and the sun shines all the day long. I search frantically at times in Bible and magazine and book for the answers to my doubts. I want assurance from Thee that mine *is* the right way, that mine *is* the right will.

I stand in need before Thee. Teach me to give, not to get. Teach me the inner peace that endures in time of storm when there is no song in the land, no beauty in the world, no sun in the sky. Teach me to live by the faith I now have, that I may be worthy of the faith Thou hast for me. Teach me *Thy* way and *Thy* will, that I may follow them.

When I consider thy heavens, the work of thy fingers, the moon and the stars, which thou hast ordained; what is man, that thou art mindful of him? and the son of man, that thou visiteth him?

Strip me, Oh God, of all that separates me from Thee, and give me that which will unite me to Thee. Strip me of myself and give me Thyself. [Fifteenth-century Swiss.]

THE PAPER

THE USE OF SILENCE

Silence, either by ourselves or with others, is strange to most of us. We do not know how to use it in our devotional life. Yet only a single time of being silent with a group of people, for fifteen minutes, for half an hour, does something to us. We begin to see the value of the discipline of silence.

Silence is for prayer and meditation. We are in the presence of God. But a barrier to our realizing His presence is our bodily tension. Sit squarely on the chair, with both feet on the floor. To be perched on the edge of a chair, with feet separated for a quick rising, is all right for one alert for possible hasty action. But we wait before the Eternal. He does not speak to hurried folk. Our bodies must be still, that our minds and spirits may be still before Him.

When we have become still, and our breathing is regular, pray in quiet the Lord's Prayer, saying each phrase slowly and with meaning. Here we will have trouble with concentration, for our mind will probably start to wander. So long have we prayed the Lord's Prayer in haste, or without thinking, that it is easy for most of us to forget what we are saying. If we find we have wandered, do not pick up the prayer where we left off; go back to the very beginning.

This is a real discipline, but in a short time we will find that we can really pray the Lord's Prayer, not just "say" it.

Now let us turn to our directed meditation (if we are in the chapel) and read it carefully. Or if we are at home, let us read a Biblical passage, a page or chapter from a devotional book, or the like. Read slowly and carefully, thinking about each idea, making it your own for the moment. Try to assume the mood of the writing. Do not argue with it, or reject it. Let it speak to you. When we find a thought worth dwelling with, do as St. Francis de Sales suggests: stay with it, look at it from different sides, ponder on it, make it come alive, before passing on to a second thought; "stay there without passing on to another, acting like the bees, who do not leave a flower so long as they find any honey there to gather" (From *Introduction to a Devout Life*).

(This warning should be made. The time of silence is not a time for study, not even of ways and techniques for prayer nor of understanding the Bible. Such books should be read at other free times. Prayer itself, and meditation on a single thought or two, by which God may speak to us, are the two essential parts of our silence or quiet time. Ancient and modern devotional classics and portions of the Scriptures are the best reading for this period.)

After we have gathered all the honey there is in "the flower" of our meditation, then move on to our prayers of intercession. Remember each person in our fellowship group, and seek God's blessing upon the service of worship for the coming Sunday. Add to our list from time to time folk who need our help. It will be inevitable for us to add those in our own homes regularly.

Do not forget our own daily commitment to Him, that His will be done each day in us. Go then from the time of silence with a thought for the day, something to brood over, a resolution to follow. St. Francis de Sales here suggests that we gather spiritual nose-gays:

Those who have been walking in a beautiful garden do not leave it willingly without taking away with them four or five flowers in order to inhale their perfume and carry them about during the day: even so, when we have considered some mystery in meditation, we should choose one or two or three points in which we have found most relish . . .

in order to remember them throughout the day, and to inhale their perfume spiritually.[1]

4

The Fourth Week

THE MEDITATION

"Not of my own will am I here, not of my own will shall I soon pass hence. Of all that shall come to me this day, very little will be such as I have chosen for myself. It is Thou, O hidden One, who dost appoint my lot and determine the bounds of my habitation."[2]

Then am I not a free person? Is it impossible for me to do as I please? Certainly I cannot choose my parents, nor my brothers and sisters. Nor can I finally put aside the day of my departure. I am what I am in body and mind and spirit because of the long line of those whose blood is in my veins.

But God has given me the freedom of choice. I can choose my friends. I can choose my attitude toward my work. I can accept or reject His way of love and inner peace. If I want not to do so, even the Eternal Father will not make me give up self to turn toward Him. He puts me in this day, with its privileges, its joys, its responsibilities, its failures, its sorrows. What I do with them is my own free will.

Yet I believe that in the midst of my freedom the voice of the Eternal God speaks to me. His providence brings me friends and opportunities. Strangely does He open for me closed doors. Strangely does He put my feet on new paths. If I will put my trust in His leading, using all of my mind and my heart and my strength to

---

[1] Francis de Sales: *Introduction to the Devout Life* (New York: Harper & Brothers), p. 48.

[2] John Baillie: A *Diary of Private Prayer* (New York: Charles Scribner's Sons, 1936), p. 41.

know His will for me, I believe I may know the true freedom of those who serve Him.

THE PAPER

EJACULATORY OR FLASH PRAYERS

As spiritual athletes we should "flex our muscles" many times through the day. Our daily period of solitude and silence has meaning only as it is surrounded by these continual spiritual exercises, known as ejaculatory prayers. "Ejaculatory"—from the "jacula" or "spear," thrust ahead—a prayer tossed ahead as though hurled from the heart toward God above. Dr. Frank Laubach and others today speak of "flash" prayers, the sudden illumination of the flash gun in taking of a photo. These are both the same, quick, brief prayers lifting self or friend before God.

These need not take us away from our work of the moment, though if we can find time for a minute rest period to sit quietly and think inwardly several times a day, recalling God and His love revealed to us in Nature, in His creatures, in His children, in the places and objects of our common day, that spiritual retirement will do far more for us than the mere "pause that refreshes."

In the following ways, and many more, we may exercise through ejaculatory prayers:

1. Before meeting a friend—

After giving the phone number to the operator, after pushing the doorbell, after the receptionist has sent you into the office, upon sight of the friend coming toward you or waiting for you, OFFER a brief prayer of thanksgiving, of blessing, for that friend and for God's spirit to rest upon your fellowship together.

2. Upon entering a shop or office—

Before speaking to the clerk or agent or salesman with whom you would deal, before asking for the person you seek, OFFER a prayer requesting God's love and light to rest upon the person you are to talk with.

3. While working at home or school or business—

As a colleague walks up to you, a neighbor rings your bell, a friend hangs her laundry in a near-by yard, a customer seeks to buy, a teacher asks a question, OFFER a prayer of praise or blessing that God's peace may rest upon this person.

4. In the many minutes of idle waiting—

While the cook vessel is coming to a boil, the iron heats, the fountain pen is filling, the chimes of the clock are striking, the operator is seeking to locate your party, the bus is late, the traffic signal halts your car, the crowd beats you to the corner store or to the ticket window, OFFER your many prayers of intercession and petition.

Eyes need never be closed for these prayers, for they are thrusts of the Spirit that rush toward God, flashes of His light that illumine our relationships. Seldom would we wish to memorize prayers to use at times like these, for they are the longings of our hearts that God's love may surround our every moment, with Him, with others.

Now in this exercise of spiritual retirement and ejaculatory prayers lies the great work of devotion: it can supply the lack of all other prayers, but the failure of this can scarcely be made good by any other means. Without it the contemplative life cannot be properly followed, nor the active life lived otherwise than ill; without it repose is but idleness, and work but embarrassment.[3]

5

The Fifth Week

THE MEDITATION

"Give us this day our daily bread." But I must put away a bit for the morrow. I can't expect anyone else to care for me. I must save now, lest I have nothing when the morrow comes. Who would take care of me then?

"Sufficient unto the day is the evil thereof." But foresight is a good thing. If I worry about what is to happen, I can prepare my-

[3] Francis de Sales: *op. cit.*, p. 59.

self for it when it comes. I can see just what is going to happen, and I am afraid even today.

"O ye of little faith." But I must be practical. I just can't live day by day and step by step. I want to see more than a step ahead, more than a day ahead. I don't want to take any chances.

"I believe, help thou mine unbelief." Thou art my Father, and I am Thy child. I put my hand in Thine. Help me to see Thy great love for me, that my worry may be ended, my fear put away. Thou dost care for me as a Father carest for His child. I thank Thee, thank Thee, thank Thee, Lord.

The Paper

THE WAY OF COMMITMENT

Commitment is a relationship, a giving of one's whole being to Someone or to a cause. It is the total obedience and devotion of a Communist to his party, of a scientist to his science, of an artist to his art. For the Christian COMMITMENT is "the life of absolute and complete and holy obedience to the voice of the Shepherd" (Thomas Kelly).

It is mature abandonment of one's entire life to God "that in advance accepts willingly the consequences involved regardless of what they may turn out to be" (Douglas Steere). Thomas a Kempis suggests the daily testings that help such abandonment:

You must often do the things you do not like; and the things you do like you must leave undone. What pleases others will succeed; what pleases you will be a failure. What others say will be listened to; but what you say will be accounted as nothing. Others ask and receive; you ask and remain unheard. Others are praised by men; you are passed over in silence. Others are assigned to one position or another; but you are accounted fit for nothing. Although you bear it in silence your nature will sometimes grieve at this and cause no small struggle within you. In these and many other things, the faithful servant of God is tested how far he can renounce himself and break his own will in all things.[1]

Now why are these humiliations a good thing? Because we must

[1] Thomas a Kempis: *The Imitation of Christ*, quoted in Douglas V. Steere, *Doors Into Life* (New York: Harper & Brothers, 1948), pp. 47–48.

learn abandonment to God, whole obedience to Him instead of to ourselves. So a Kempis says further:

It is good for us that we sometimes suffer contradictions and that we are misjudged even when we do what is right. Such humiliations may shield us from vainglory. For when a man of good will is downtrodden and outwardly despised and discredited or when he is tormented with evil intentions within, then he realizes that he has greater need of God without whom he can do nothing.

Commitment thus involves first of all, GOD. "One can give oneself only to something which is there, which can be observed, understood and obeyed; to something which makes demands and holds out promises and obligations." [2] Then second comes the act of commitment, "Ye must be born again"; "If any man is in Christ, he is a new creature." Third, it involves humility, a deep humility, for

The committed Christian does not claim to have arrived; he is, instead, willing to start. He is, accordingly, perplexed, but not unto despair. He knows that at best we touch only the fringe of the divine garment and that even the little we see is seen through a glass darkly, but he is unwilling, for that reason, to fall back into sceptical futility. He has seen a tiny light and that light he will follow, even though he does not know all the answers.[3]

In this alone do we find true wholeness, that which Jesus meant when he said: "Be ye perfect, even as your Father in heaven is perfect." Thomas Kelly says:

The life that intends to be wholly obedient, wholly submissive, wholly listening, is astonishing in its completeness. Its joys are ravishing, its peace profound, its humility the deepest, its power world-shaking, its love enveloping, its simplicity that of a trusting child.

For most of us commitment is a step-by-step procedure by which we struggle continually to know God's will for us through complete obedience to Him. Thomas Kelly suggests four steps by which we

[2] Gregory Vlastos, quoted in The Choice Is Always Ours, ed. by Phillips (New York: Richard R. Smith, 1948), p. 27.
[3] D. Elton Trueblood: Alternative to Futility (New York: Harper & Brothers, 1947), pp. 63–64.

move forward.[4] *First* is "The flaming vision of the wonder of such a life." It may be rather prosaic in its beginning, a suggestion rather than a deep urge, that comes through a book we are reading, a life we see lived before us, a Biblical verse that touches us, through an experience by which we know for certain God strangely has touched our life. With this "vision" behind us, commonplace or ecstatic though it may be, known at the time or recognized only after some interval has passed, we are ready to move forward.

Second step to commitment is "Begin where you are. Obey *now*." Using the little commitment which we are capable of, moment by moment continually offer ourselves in continuous obedience, keeping up a silent prayer: "Open Thou my life. Guide my thoughts where I dare not let them go. But Thou darest. Thy will be done." Kelly says he finds this

internal continuous prayer life absolutely essential. It can be carried on day and night, in the thick of business, in home and school. Such prayer of submission can be so simple. It is well to use a single sentence, repeated over and over and over again, such as this: "Be Thou my will. Be Thou my will," or "I open all before Thee. I open all before Thee," or "See earth through heaven. See earth through heaven." This hidden prayer life can pass, in time beyond words and phrases into mere ejaculations, "My God, my God, my Holy One, my Love."

Third step to commitment is this:

If you slip and stumble and forget God for an hour, and assert your old proud self, and rely upon your own clever wisdom, don't spend too much time in anguished regrets and self-accusations but begin again, just where you are.

Fourth step is this:

Don't grit your teeth and clench your fists and say, "I will! I will!" Relax. Take hands off. Submit yourself to God. Learn to live in the passive voice—a hard saying for an American—and let life be willed through you. For "I will" spells not obedience.

Kelly also suggests the fruits of holy obedience or commitment. First, there is a sense of utter humility that "rests upon the dis-

---

[4] Thomas Kelly: *op. cit.*, chapter on "Holy Obedience," pp. 51 ff.

closure of the consummate wonder of God, upon finding that only God counts, that all our own self-originated intentions are works of straw." He further says: "Growth in humility is a measure of our growth in the habit of the God-directed mind. . . ." "Utter obedience is self-forgetful obedience." "If we live in complete humility in God we can smile in patient assurance as we work."

The second fruit is a passion for personal holiness.

One burns for complete innocency and holiness of personal life. No man can look on God and live, live in his own faults, live in the shadow of the least self-deceit, live in harm toward His least creatures, whether man, or bird or beast or creeping thing. . . . For the life of obedience is a holy life, a separated life, a renounced life, cut off from worldly compromises, distinct, heaven-dedicated in the midst of men, stainless as the snows upon the mountain tops.

Third of the fruits is entrance into suffering. The soul made sensitive through complete abandonment to God knows suffering as no other does.

The heart is stretched through suffering, and enlarged. But O the agony of this enlarging of the heart, that one may be prepared to enter into the anguish of others! Yet the way of holy obedience leads out from the heart of God and extends through the Valley of the Shadow.

The last fruit of commitment, as Kelly suggests it, is

the simplicity of the trusting child, the simplicity of the children of God . . . It is the beginning of spiritual maturity, which comes after the awkward age of religious busyness for the Kingdom of God . . . knowing sorrow to the depths it does not agonize and fret and strain, but in serene, unhurried calm it walks in time with the joy and assurance of Eternity. . . . For the simplified man loves God with all his heart and mind and soul and strength and abides trustingly in that love. Then indeed we love our neighbors. And the Fellowship of the Horny Hands is identical with the Fellowship of the Transfigured Face, in this Mary-Martha life.

6

The Sixth Week

THE MEDITATION

In this place made holy to me because of silence that speaks of Thee and fellowship that warms my heart, I feel Thy presence. Thou art in my very being, and I lift my eyes in thanksgiving to Thee. I do not fear, for Thou art with me; I am not dismayed for Thou art my God; Thou dost indeed give me strength and help and Thy right hand to lead me. Bless the Lord, O my soul, and all that is within me, bless His Holy Name.

I am not alone. The Spirit of the Eternal Christ is here, brooding over me as long ago he sought to brood over the people of Jerusalem. I feel his hand upon my heart. Saints of old, men and women of my childhood and growing days, parents or teachers or friends who knew Thee, are pleased to be with me in spirit right now. I remember —— and ——, who would be so glad to sit next to me in the flesh, if they could. How deep would be our fellowship together! For Thou didst give them Love, which they gave without restraint to me.

I am not alone. Here with me are friends who know Thy presence, who feel Thy moving spirit. From their cup of joy I unfilled would drink. From their bread of sharing I unfed would eat. Here I give to Thee the little I have, my small loaves and my few fishes. Spread them upon Thy table, where all may take.

> And so I find it well to come
> For deeper rest to this still room,
> For here the habit of the soul
> Feels less the outer world's control;
> The strength of mutual purpose pleads

More earnestly our common needs;
And from the silence multiplied
By these still forms on either side
The world that time and sense have known
Falls off and leaves us God alone.

                                        (Whittier)

THE PAPER

HELPS FOR MEDITATION

A meditation is a reading with a set theme, in which the reader continually is asking himself: "What is God saying to ME through this reading?" Then follows the important question: "What changes in my life must come because of this reading?" Hence, "meditation brings us into an encounter, a taking position toward, a coming into personal change by reason of that which we meditate upon" (Douglas Steere). So, out of the considerations and the resolutions: "For example, if I have resolved"—in the meditation period—"to win by gentleness the hearts of those who offend me, I will seek that very day an opportunity of meeting them in order to greet them amicably; if I fail to meet them, I at least will try to speak well of them and pray to God on their behalf" (St. Francis de Sales).

Choose then one point of interest, the set theme of the meditation, letting the mind take hold of it, ideas and feelings flowing out of it. Sooner or later the theme will become alive, a new thought and new will to act in its light.

To choose one's own meditation, follow one or more of these ways:

1. Read a Biblical passage, and with imagination take part in it as though an onlooker. For example, consider Jesus cleansing the temple (Mark 11:15–18) and see him casting out buyers and sellers, feel their fear and indignation, watch the spilt money go rolling, hear him telling the people the temple is to be a house of prayer. Why was it made a "den of thieves"? Why did he do what he did? How have I made the Church a commercial institution, instead of a house of prayer? Resolve to act as God suggests in this imaginative understanding of the incident. Stay with the medita-

tion long enough to find one true resolution to touch your life, then move on.

2. Read a prepared meditation or prayer, considering how it relates to one's own life, following its consideration with like resolutions. Then move on. (Use John Baillie, A *Diary of Private Prayer*; W. E. Orchard, *The Temple*; Philippe Vernier, *Not as the World Giveth*; or any daily devotional guide or the like.)

3. Choose a word or a phrase, and write or think through one's own meditation, using "The Love of God," "Christian Hope," "The Peace of God," "Forgiveness," "The Abiding Presence of God," "Sin," "Death," "The Providence of God," "Creative Power," "Serenity," "Patience," "God's Purpose for Me," "Christian Fellowship" and the like.

4. Use a symbol from art, a painting, a poem, a hymn, a bit of music, before which one sits quietly, absorbing what God says to us through it, resolving that the Reality revealed there will find expression in our daily living.

5. Prepare one's own meditation from a "holy sentence," which may be a text from the Bible, a couplet or line from a favorite poem, a sentence from one's own anthology of meaningful words, such as the following:

He give me a orange once when little,
And he who gives a child a treat
Makes joy-bells ring in Heaven's street. [Masefield]

You can lose a man like that by your own death, but not by his. [Shaw of Morris]

I liked that big room at Tyn-y-Coed. It was high, and the windows big and plenty of them, planned in a day when men thought spaciously and lived graciously, and had a love for good work. [Llewellyn, *How Green Was My Valley*]

I don't believe it. Nobody's ever going to fly; and if anybody did fly, it wouldn't be anybody from Dayton. [In 1903, Dayton man hearing of the Wright brothers]

Give me the patience to accept those things which cannot be changed, the courage to change those things which can be changed, and the wisdom to know the difference. [Unknown]

Every event is a creative opportunity, every contact is an insight, a revelation. [Anonymous]

7

The Seventh Week

THE MEDITATION

Counting himself nothing before God, the Apostle Paul yet could say, "I can do all things through Christ which strengtheneth me." If I would follow Christ I must come to this same twofold belief: a complete humility that recognizes my own inadequacy and a complete assurance and confidence that recognizes God's amazing use of me.

I have a good mind, a background of fine experience, a native ability, that is not to be denied. I am not a self-made person, but I certainly have done wonders with what little I had to start with. Yet before the Eternal God, I must face these inevitable questions:

Why am I embarrassed at times, and a failure often, in witnessing for Him?

Why do so many little things, counted even by me to be insignificant, make me irritable, and frequently ill-tempered?

How have I given my talents, small though they may be, to be used by him?

Where do I do even my rightful share of His work in my own Church?

How much has the heavy hand of pride pulled me away from His presence?

What do I really know about the amazing love of God, and what have I done about it?

Deep within my own heart, am I proud of my service for Him?

Yet when I abandon myself wholly to Him, how remarkable, how amazing, how almost unbelievable is His use of my life! Through me someone has found a rock upon which to rest his faith. Through me someone has learned what friendliness can mean. Through me someone has found courage and strength to hold fast to good and God. My voice He has taken, my hands He has used, my feet He has followed, my ears He has listened with, my heart He has won.

THE PAPER

INTERCESSORY PRAYER

From the beginning of the Christian faith prayer for others has been at its heart. It was the practice of Jesus, of Paul, of the saints of the early days of the Church, and down through the generations men and women have continued to intercede with God for people and for causes. Yet no problem of prayer for one believing in its power is so frequent as the question: How can my prayer for someone else, especially one at a distance who knows nothing of my prayer, be at all meaningful, except to me?

There is no answer that will satisfy completely. There is strange coincidence that cannot be explained by scientific fact which makes one think that prayer does cross all boundaries of time and space. But there is no "quantitative" proof for this, nor any scientific measurement.

One must either accept the way of Jesus and the saints through the years as a theory by which to pray, or one must discard this way. Neither accepting nor rejecting can be based on measured proof. Either must be taken without knowing all the answers of the mystery of God's providence and mercy. But the saints through the years, and even in this time, refuse to let any failure of measurable proof prevent them from taking part in the unselfish, creative act of bringing persons and causes before God.

Aldous Huxley suggests that intercession is "the means to, and the expression of, the love of one's neighbor." Praying for another person, friend or foe, or praying for a cause, is so unselsh an act that its sincerity means a changed relationship.

To pray for another:

By considering yourself as an advocate with God for your neighbours and acquaintances, you would never find it hard to be at peace with them yourself. It would be easy for you to bear with and forgive those, for whom you particularly implored the divine mercy and forgiveness. . . .

Intercession is the best arbitrator of all differences, the best promoter of true friendship, the best cure and preservative against all unkind tempers, all angry and haughty passions.[1]

You cannot possibly have any ill-temper, or show any unkind behaviour to a man for whose welfare you are so much concerned, as to be his advocate with God in private. For you cannot possibly despise and ridicule that man whom your private prayers recommend to the love and favour of God.[2]

To pray for a cause:

A frequent intercession with God, earnestly beseeching him to forgive the sins of all mankind, to bless them with his providence, enlighten them with his Spirit, and bring them to everlasting happiness, is the divinest exercise that the heart of man can be engaged in. Be daily therefore on your knees, in a solemn, deliberate performance of this devotion, and you will find all little, ill-natured passions die away, your heart grow great and generous, delighting in the common happiness of others, as you used only to delight in your own. This is the natural effect of a general intercession for all mankind.

Thus we are to treat all mankind as neighbours and brethren, as any occasion offers: yet as we can only live in the actual society of a few, therefore you should always change and alter your intercessions, according as the needs and necessities of your neighbours or acquaintances seem to require: such intercessions, besides the great charity of them, would have a mighty effect upon your own heart for *there is nothing that makes us love a man so much, as praying for him*. That will give you a better and sweeter behaviour than anything that is called fine breeding and good manners.[3]

[1] William Law, quoted in *The Perennial Philosophy* by Aldous Huxley (New York: Harper & Brothers, 1945), p. 222.
[2] *Ibid.*, p. 223.
[3] William Law, quoted in *The Choice Is Always Ours*, pp. 272–273.

8

The Eighth Week

THE MEDITATION

Not alone do I sit here in the silence. My best thoughts and my best hopes are not centered in my Best Self alone. I am confronted by the Eternal God. I stand as one naked in His presence.

Nor do I find in fellowship with others in this place of silence the source of my strength. Beyond the unity that draws us together, beyond the outreaching of one for the other, beyond the sharing of heart and mind, fine as these are, is the Eternal God. He is my Judge. He is my Forgiving Lover. He is my Saviour.

My highest thoughts are not fine enough for me to seek praise for myself, nor fine enough to keep me from pride in accomplishment. My friends, even these within this rich fellowship, are not fine enough to bring to me the fullest happiness. This can come only as I go beyond self, beyond friends, to Thee.

I do stand before Thee, O Eternal One. I am selfish, thoughtless, afraid, sinful. I confess the evil of my way, doing what I should not do, and not doing what I should do. I always do the right thing, it seems, but at the wrong time! Yet, unbelievable though it may be, Thou dost continually forgive me. Thou dost call me to turn from my past, to face unafraid the future, as I live just this day. I would sing Thy praise, for Thou dost speak peace to my heavy heart. I would bless Thy Holy Name, for Thou dost speak peace to my confused mind.

Now take me and use me to be wholly Thine. I would make myself the best I can be, physically, mentally, spiritually, for Thee. I would choose the friends through whom I best can know Thee and Thy love. The worst that is in me, and the best that I have, all I give unto Thee. Cleanse me of self, that I may be Thine.

The Paper

SPIRITUAL DRYNESS

Discouragement is inevitable in the beginning of our practice of the presence of God. Time and time again we will wonder if there is any worth in continuing. We seem to be making such little headway against the winds of doubt and dissatisfaction. But this is not a condition peculiar to us. All the saints through the years have known it.

It may be puzzlement because our way of commitment is not that of the world. We may feel as though we should forget the way of Christ and return to the way of the world. Or we may be disturbed because we seemingly are not receiving the ecstasy of spirit that we thought would come to us in our commitment. Life becomes humdrum once again, and our first joy wears thin. Or we may in our creatureliness decide that after all we cannot approach the Living God. We are but human beings, and His Holy Spirit is far beyond us. We can only hope that somehow in our finiteness we may find a sense of peace and brotherliness.

Baron Von Hügel gives three simple images [1] that have helped him along "many a flinty furlong." Remember in time of dryness

that I would be climbing a mountain where, off and on, I might be enveloped in mist for days on end, unable to see a foot before me. Had I noticed how mountaineers climb mountains? How they have a quiet, regular, short step—on the level it looks petty; but then this step they keep up, on and on as they ascend, whilst the inexperienced townsman hurries along, and soon has to stop, dead beat with the climb. That such an expert mountaineer, when the thick mists come, halts and camps out under some slight cover brought with him, quietly smoking his pipe, and moving on only when the mist has cleared away.

Then remember when making a sea voyage with storms ahead,

how I must now select, and fix in my little cabin, some few but entirely appropriate things—a small trunk fixed up at one end, a chair that would keep its position, tumbler and glass that would do ditto: all this, simple, strong and selected throughout in view of stormy weather.

[1] Douglas V. Steere: *Doors into Life* (New York: Harper & Brothers, 1948), pp. 182–183.

And third,

I am travelling in a camel across a huge desert. Windless days occur and then all is well. But hurricane of wind will come, unforeseen, tremendous. What to do then? . . . Dismount from the camel, fall prostrate face downwards on the sand, covering your head with your cloak. And lie thus, an hour, three hours, half a day; the sand storm will go, and you will arise, and continue your journey as if nothing had happened.

Causes of spiritual dryness:

1. We may be traveling too fast, wanting to hurry God's spirit, praying, Give me now!

2. We may be proud, glorying in our achievement, as though it were ours.

3. We may forget our discipline, putting off our quiet time from early morning to a later period, or even missing it entirely; or may become casual in it.

4. We may be insincere, seeking our own gains and pleasures, instead of His will.

5. We may be seeking largely material gains, wealth, health, friends, reputation and so on, so that our spiritual desires are pushed into a corner of our lives.

6. We may be too eager for the new, forgetting the blessings which have come to us from past experience, instead of resting in His love until the new is opened up.

Helps to overcome spiritual dryness:

1. By examination see if the cause rests in ourselves. If so, pray that it may be put away through the grace of God, resolving to obey His guidance.

2. If no known cause is brought to mind, turn away from questioning to affirming the joy and love of God, humbling ourselves before His goodness.

3. Continue faithfully, with even stricter discipline, perhaps returning to vocal prayer, the observance of the quiet time. Write out meditations upon the blessing that has come through the love of God in times past.

4. Pray increasingly for others, making intercessory prayer your major prayers.

5. Reach out in love to serve others, going out of the way to do this.

The Ninth Week

THE MEDITATION

"Every time I feel de spirit, Movin' in my heart, I will pray."

Yes, this Negro spiritual speaks the truth. Not only for my own need, nor for the need of a friend, will I talk with Thee. I will lift up my heart to Thee whenever I feel the touch of Thy spirit. As my closed eyes lifted to the light feel its warm brightness, so my closed heart lifted to Thee feels Thy spirit. I would open my heart to Thee.

Sometimes I try to hush Thy voice. Sometimes I don't want to take time to listen to Thy words. Sometimes I don't want to be bothered to do what I am told to do. The more I plug my ears the less sensitive I become to Thy whisper. Yet Thou dost not turn from me. With yearning Thou dost speak to me.

Warm me with the fire of Thy spirit that the ice of my heart may melt before Thee. Lengthen the antennae of my inner ear that I may tune in Thy least call. Then will I lift up my heart unto Thee. Then will I raise my voice in glad praise.

"Every time I feel de spirit, Movin' in my heart, I *will* pray."

THE PAPER

PHYSICAL AND MENTAL RELAXATION

Miss Muriel Lester, noted English settlement house worker, peace advocate and humble exponent of prayer, was told by her doctor that she would not live long because of her nervous exhaustion until she took a complete and total rest, ending all her activity. Instead, she worked out a system of relaxation, so that now fifty years later she is still alive, still traveling over the world, still help-ing many groups find inner resources.

For our purposes the steps she used are adapted as follows:

First, find a room where one can be undisturbed for at least an hour. Lock the door or otherwise make certain of no disturb-ance.

Second, lie down on one's back either on a very hard bed or preferably upon a carpet or blanket on the floor.

Third, begin with the right hand to unloosen the muscles of fingers and wrist. As soon as the hand is limp and relaxed, then do the same for the entire arm. Go on to the left hand and left arm in like manner. Follow this with the right foot and leg, the left foot and leg.

Fourth, by this time the hands and arms for most of us will be quite tense again. So start all over again, right hand and arm, left hand and arm, right foot and leg, left foot and leg. It may be necessary to repeat this entire procedure three or four or more times until all are relaxed and still.

Fifth, if the neck muscles have not by this time relaxed, begin to loosen them. If in doing so, the other muscles tense again, go back to the beginning and repeat the entire series.

Sixth, now relax the facial muscles, especially those controlling the eyes and the mouth. By this time, perhaps fifteen minutes, perhaps longer for the first few times, a complete relaxation should have taken one, like a kitten asleep on the floor. A sense of well-being flows over the body.

Seventh, if the breathing has not already become slower and rhythmic—and it probably will have started to be thus—take deep breaths. But the relaxed body should have revealed this regularity already.

Eighth, after waiting a half hour or more in this relaxed position, resting upon the floor or bed as easily as a petal on a quiet pond, bring to mind the Lord's Prayer, the Twenty-third Psalm, the hymn "Breathe on Me, Breath of God," saying these over and over with the rhythm of one's breathing.

Ninth, hold in mind name by name those for whom you would pray, letting your peace and quiet flow out to them.

Tenth, get up at the end of an hour, relaxed in mind and spirit, a new person.

REMINDERS: Do not miss such discipline on any day. For those whose tensions are on the verge of snapping, continue without fail this daily discipline, at least an hour, until one's spirit has completely become one with the onflowing of God's spirit. This may be two weeks or two months. But keep it up until, within a minute of stretching out, one is completely relaxed. Better to use an hour like this daily, and then live for Him the rest of one's life!

When you are feeling so rested and alive that such a discipline is no longer needed, follow it anyway. After two or three months when the mind and body are completely renewed, fifteen minutes each day may be all that is needed.

10

The Tenth Week

THE MEDITATION

"Here am I! Send me." So it was the young Isaiah answered Thy call to him. So I would answer Thee myself. Call me to service, for Thy Church, for Thy nation, for Thy people. No matter what the task may be, I want to be used by Thee.

But I sit in no high council, nor does my voice carry weight among the mighty. What can I do where I am? Some task that will enlist my whole being, my mind, my heart, my body. Some task into which I can place all my energy, that I will know, and others will know, that Thou art using me!

Yet that might mean I seek renown! No, Lord, sincere I am. Then the answer may be no great place of service, but like the tired Martha, carrying on the normal work of the day.

How can I be used in my home, to be more co-operative, more thoughtful, more loving, more cheerful, less critical, less selfish?

Yea, Lord, and in what other ways may I be used by Thee right at home!

Or in my work, as Christian housewife, Christian teacher, Christian office worker, whatever it may be, how there in that place may I reveal Thy spirit? Truly I seek no high place, no great reward; I ask only that Thou wilt use me.

And if it seems wise that I should not for a time be used by Thee, take my waiting, and help me be patient. Accept my love and my intent, O Thou Eternal God.

The Paper

WHEN DISTRACTIONS INTERRUPT

Distractions are a real problem in one's quiet time. It is difficult for most folk to hold to one thought for any length of time. We are so far away from formal schooling, the last times that we really practiced concentration, that the mind readily wanders. Hence, any little distraction will start the mind wandering. What then should we do?

Before anything else, we should check our conscience. Is something bothering us, because of wrong thought or wrong action? If we are angry toward someone, resentful or jealous; or if we have been spiteful toward someone, speaking sharply or with lashing tongue, we will find it almost impossible to concentrate upon our meditation and prayer. That wrong thought or that wrong action is going to come to the fore. It must be faced sincerely. Wrongs must be righted, forgiveness sought, before we will find it possible to meditate freely.

But if one's conscience is clear, there are still several reasons for distractions. For one thing, if one has no theme for his meditation, his mind inevitably will wander. Just to sit quietly with nothing to hold one's attention will be most confusing to the beginner. (Later, for one trained in prayer, a theme for meditation will not be necessary much of the time; but most of us have not reached that stage of growth.) For the beginner there must be a theme of some kind. It may be a passage from the Bible or some devotional book, a stanza from a hymn, a phrase from one's notebook, a picture or symbol or portion of music—there are many sources from which to choose. Having a theme means a chance to center one's thoughts. (Go back to the paper for the Sixth Week, "Helps for Meditation," for suggestions at this point.)

Sometimes the theme may be too large, too varied. One's thoughts then are far too scattered. The theme should be narrowed to a single point, with which one may dwell profitably. For example, the theme "The Love of God" is too large for most of us, great and vast as it is. Break it down into smaller parts, such as the love of God as revealed through a friend, or in the fellowship of a church, or in the parable of the Prodigal Son, or another such phase of the larger subject. Each one of these is worthy of a period of uninterrupted meditation. But too vast a theme only leads to distracting thoughts, scattered because of disunity.

Then again, outside interruptions come. A workman is noisy just beyond one's quiet room, or the voices of children at play may be heard. Do not push these interruptions away. Bring them into the meditation. Ask God's blessing upon the workman, upon the children, upon the salesman who calls at the door, upon the friend who phones in the midst of the quiet time. To drive these folk aside with irritation (after all, don't they know I'm trying to listen to God!) will only hinder one's search for God. But after these folk have been brought into the quiet time, then return once more to the subject of the meditation.

Here is where we need patience. Do not be discouraged when the mind wanders or there are distractions such as mentioned above. Go back to the original theme. If another interruption comes, again go back to the meditation. Do not give up the quiet time. Do not wait for fewer interruptions. Do not wait for another day to continue your meditation. Right there and then, persistently return, again and again if need be, to the theme. Gradually one will find that persistent returning to the theme is the finest way to lessen distractions.

But above all, remember that the meditation, even the quiet time, is not an end in itself. It is a time of silence to bring us into the presence of God. If at the end of a few minutes there is a sudden awareness of the Spirit of God, drop the meditation. Just rest in that awareness of Him. The purpose of the meditation has been achieved! As soon as the quiet time is ended, go out into the day's activity carrying that awareness into every bit of it. Let whatever is done be interspersed with flash prayers of thanksgiving and adoration. Then return the next day to the quiet time, prepared to meet distractions courageously as they may come.

11

The Eleventh Week

THE MEDITATION

Naaman was a great general, but he had leprosy. His wife's little slave girl, captured from Samaria in Israel, told him a prophet in Samaria could heal him. So Naaman of Syria, with a host of slaves and many gifts, went to see Elisha, the man of God. To the mighty general Elisha sent a simple word: "Go and wash in Jordan seven times."

But Naaman was angry. Was he not a great general? Did the prophet dare despise him by sending out a servant instead of coming himself to him? And should he do so simple and matter-of-fact a thing as to wash seven times in the River Jordan? Why! He had bigger and better rivers at home! So Naaman turned away in his anger.

But the servants of Naaman were wise. To him they said, "If the prophet had bid thee do some great thing, wouldst thou not have done it?" So Naaman dipped himself in the Jordan and was healed.

Is it so, Lord, that Thou dost speak to me? My healing, my peace of mind and heart and soul, do these come from following the least of Thy commands? But Thou knowest I do love Thee, and I would serve Thee with great service! I want to be doing something important for Thee. Let me choose it, so it will be a great thing!

But then it will be my choosing, and not Thine! Perhaps it is my glory I seek, a fine reputation, public acclaim, instead of Thy glory! Forgive me, O God of love. Speak to me of little things that doing them I may find myself worthy someday of doing great things for Thee!

THE PAPER

LOVE IN ACTION

If we forget everything else Jesus ever said, but remember one word, we have after all what he himself said was the all important: Thou shalt love the Lord thy God with all thy heart and all thy mind and all thy soul and all thy strength; and thou shalt love thy neighbor as thyself.

But either one left alone is dangerous. Just to love God may lead one into quiet places apart from the stream of life. Just to love one's neighbor may lead one into human activity that is without foundation. Love in action is the continual merging of the two; love of God revealed in the fruits of one's life, and love of neighbor founded upon one's relationship to the Eternal God.

So, when St. Francis of Assisi led some followers into Holy Orders, he also founded "The Third Order" for those who would remain in the world, but not of the world. He had only one rule: "To make restitution of all ill-gotten gains, to become reconciled with his enemies, to live in peace and concord with all men, to pass his life in prayer and works of charity, to keep certain fasts and vigils, to pay tithes regularly to the Church, to take no oath save under exceptional conditions, never to wear arms, to use no foul language, and to practice piety to the dead." This all came out of complete devotion and commitment to God, which was to bear fruit thus.

Now, our actions will be twofold: first, the quiet, neighborly deeds of everyday living; and second, the deep concerns of racial and economic and international brotherhood. De Caussade writes that "There is no one in the world who cannot arrive without difficulty at the most eminent perfection by fulfilling with love obscure and common duties." He who seeks only the large things will direct himself away from God. Beginning with what we are and with what we have and with the place in which we live, He calls us to share with others our relationship of peace and love that we have found in Him. So Fritz Kunkel suggests how we may begin at home, then find ourselves gradually coming into the larger concern.

Expose yourself to situations in which you are stirred by genuine understanding and sympathy, in which you feel a desire to cooperate with and help another regardless of material or other reward than your inner We-feeling satisfaction. Learn from first-hand observation something of the life of those less-favourably situated than you are. Seek an opportunity for some volunteer service to the sick, the needy, the oppressed. Visit some shut-in and read aloud awhile or otherwise share his load. Find a way to understand better the unhappiness of someone oppressed by racial prejudice or social injustice. Look for the shy person to whom you can be friendly. Give a lift to your tired fellow-worker. Let your imagination lead you into some We-feeling response to those far away—perhaps the starving men in Europe, in Asia or the flood victim in your own country. These are but a fraction of the possibilities which may be discovered.[1]

Then it is we are ready to be chosen by God for action in the deeper concerns. Let us not rush into this and that, but out of our prayer and our vision, let us choose the door for action which He opens for us. Wait patiently until the door is open, for He will do it in His own time. Rose Terlin says: "Prayer is not escape from reality and from action; it is the source of strength and insight for action. It is the only preparation for sound action."[2]

Out of this quiet contemplation comes our love in action. Again, let us understand we must begin where we are with what we have. As Philippe Vernier well says:

Therefore do not wait for great strength before setting out, for immobility will weaken you further. Do not wait to see very clearly before starting: one has to walk toward the light. Have you strength enough to take this first step? Courage enough to accomplish this little tiny act of fidelity or reparation, the necessity of which is apparent to you? Take this step! perform this act! You will be astonished to feel that the effort accomplished, instead of having exhausted your strength,

[1] Fritz Kunkel, quoted in *The Choice Is Always Ours*, p. 360.
[2] Rose Terlin, quoted in *The Choice Is Always Ours*, p. 351.

has doubled it, and that you already see more clearly what you have to do next.[3]

12

The Twelfth Week

The Meditation

What makes me angry? Deep within there is a burning fire because of the seemingly futile waste of life in war, or because of the continued prejudice toward children of Thine of color or race or creed different from mine. But this anger strengthens my conviction to help all who need my help. It clears my mind to study further how I may be used by Thee. It makes me more determined to hold all men as brothers.

But I get angry in ways that destroy my inner being. I flare out against someone who judges me wrongly. Why doesn't that person try to see my side of things? (Though I wonder if I always try to see the other person's point of view?) Or I become peeved because I do not get the just recognition I deserve. Thou knowest I do not want any praise I do not earn. But I am so often accepted casually, and my work that takes the greatest preparation is brushed aside carelessly.

Then there comes the time when my family fails to understand me. I'm busy about my work and I don't get help when I need it; or I'm in a hurry to go to a meeting, and no one offers to help me get ready to go. Sometimes I get tired, and I don't mean to speak sharply or crossly; but I get upset and the entire household is restless.

Help me, O Thou Great Physician, so to watch my health that late nights and hurried work will not make me prone to irritation. Guard me, O Thou Source of Quiet, that outward noise and con-

[3] Philippe Vernier, quoted in *The Choice Is Always Ours*, pp. 354–355

fusion will not tear the inner ear of my spirit. Watch over me, O Thou Great Judge, that I do not judge harshly or critically when seemingly I do not receive the adulation and honor I expect. Teach me, O Thou Source of all Good Laughter, my right place in life, that I be neither bloated with my importance nor stunned with my inadequacy.

THE PAPER

DISCIPLINE

We are growing in the practice of the presence of God through these fellowship groups exactly in proportion to our acceptance of discipline. If we are casual and irregular in our spiritual exercises, we miss the fullness and bounty that can be ours.

As a minimum discipline we agreed to practice the following:

1. Pray each day at least once for each person in our fellowship group.

2. Pray each day for the blessing of God upon the services of worship of the Sunday that lies ahead, for the minister, for the congregation.

Additional discipline that has proved most helpful:

1. Worship—regular sharing in public worship, a minimum of once a week. This is group sharing, lifting our hearts to God in fellowship with others.

2. Solitude—spending part of each day alone for private prayer and devotional reading. The missing of a single day quickly becomes noticeable to the person under discipline. Things happen to us in the aloneness.

3. Silence—getting the body and the mind still, to listen to the voice of God. Beginning with a minimum of fifteen minutes, we try to find at least an hour each day.

4. Love—the way of social concern, every day including some outgoing activity not for ourselves. Our exercises will be meaningless if they do not find outreach in helpfulness and friendliness, both at home and at a distance.

5. Austerity—simple living, releasing the mind from the entanglement of material interests, and releasing income for the service of God and man.

(Adapted from D. Elton Trueblood's *Alternative to Futility*.)

Others have found these two additional suggestions helpful:

1. Offer before each meal, in silence or with spoken word, a simple grace.

2. Set aside upon receipt of one's income BEFORE any portion is removed a definite proportion of that income to be used ONLY for benevolent purposes, church, Red Cross, community chest, and the like. (This should not include gifts to members of one's own family, nor expenses involved in performing charitable acts.) This is partial fulfillment of the fifth discipline above.

The Fellowship of Tithers—

In Old Testament days the tithe was the "first fruits" of crops or animals, even at times including the firstborn son. This meant giving the very best to God, not waiting until the smaller and second-rate pickings which would mean a lower price on the market or a lower quality of goods.

After the barter-methods largely passed by, and money became the medium of exchange, the system of 10 per cent tithing developed, meaning one-tenth of one's income was to be set aside before any other amount was removed from that income. In the ordinary meaning of the word today, a tithe is this 10 per cent.

For many people this has become proportionate giving, a certain percentage which may be more or less than the suggested 10 per cent, which too is set aside when the income first is received. The reason for this setting aside is simply one's belief that he is after all a steward for God, that actually he owns nothing, but that all has come through the gifts of God used by the individual. Hence, before meeting any other obligations, he will put aside the proportion for God's use in benevolences. This is a privilege, and not a duty to be enforced.

Today in one denomination there is a group known as the Fellowship of Tithers, who agree to give a minimum of 10 per cent of all their income to benevolence. They do not hold meetings, have no dues, elect no officers; but are a voluntary fellowship of men and women who sign a written agreement to share in such tithing as an expression of their Christian discipline.

13

The Thirteenth Week

The Meditation

"Eye hath not seen, nor ear heard, neither have entered into the heart of man, the things which the Lord hath prepared for those that love him."

Open my eyes that I may see. In the rising up of the sun and the glory of the day I see Thy presence. In the going down of the same and the beauty of the starry night I see Thy majesty. How marvelous are Thy works, and far beyond the understanding of man! I call to mind —— that speaks of Thee.

Open my eyes that I may see. In the little creatures of earth and sky and sea, the loyalty of a dog, the song of a bird, the shimmering of a fish, I see Thy handiwork. How often I am reminded of Thee as I watch Thy creatures at play or in flight. I call to mind —— that speaks of Thee.

Open my eyes that I may see. In the faces of people I read letters from Thee. Here is written the wisdom and strength that comes from Thee as I see it on the face of ——. On the face of —— I see the —— which Life has stamped there. I see both the gifts that have come from Thee, and the need which Thou canst meet. I call to mind the face of —— that speaks of Thee.

Open my eyes that I may see. In places and objects of my common day I am aware of Thyself. Symbols they are of man's evil and man's good in the way of Life. A mailman binding separated people together, a blaring radio and the emptiness of many lives, a police car that suggests Thy protection, a table around which a family gathers in fellowship, the open door of a church inviting the seeker to God within, a newspaper with its thrills and horors and tragedies and joys—these speak to me of Thee. I call to mind —— that speaks of Thee.

THE PAPER

MEDITATIONS THROUGH THE FIVE SENSES

Ignatius of Loyola, in his *Spiritual Exercises*, suggests a way to meditate upon the Gospel stories. Read a single incident from one of the four Gospels, using the imagination creatively, so as to understand that incident in the life of Jesus, by taking each of the five senses, one by one, as the basis of the reading and imagining.

Let us take a fairly long story, Mark 6:30–44, the feeding of the five thousand, as a sample. First, SEE the story, the apostles with eager faces telling Jesus excitedly about the experiences of their visitation (previous verses), and Jesus' eager but patient response to come into a quiet place. Then see the crowds coming, men and women in varied garb, with curious children too, and Jesus' disappointment at first, then his compassion, as he talks to them. Then, SEE the discussion about food to eat, and the collecting of the bits of food, and the arranging of the crowd in companies, and the eating of the meal, and the gathering of food afterward.

Second, HEAR the story, listening to the eager apostles and Jesus' words of encouragement. Then HEAR the group quietly going to a desert spot, and the distant clamoring, and finally, the noisy coming of the multitude. HEAR the words of Jesus as he taught, the words of the questioning about food to eat, the comments of disciples and of the crowd as Jesus blessed the food and distributed it. HEAR the people in conversation as they eat, especially the voices of the children.

Third, TOUCH the rough robes of the apostles, the staves they use as they walk along, the ministering hand of Jesus, the texture of the dried bread and cooked fish, the smooth cheeks of little children, the hard ground where all sat on the green grass.

Fourth, SMELL the fresh wind on the lake as they cross by boat, smell the warm wind in the desert spot, smell the body warmth of the multitude, smell the bread and the fish, smell the cool green grass where they sit.

Fifth, TASTE the fresh water of the lake, taste the heat of the desert spot, taste the dried bread and fish, taste the perspiration of the warm crowd.

Each story will be different. Some will have almost no suggestion for the taste sense, and a few may have little of the sense of smell. But all will have seeing and hearing and touching. With each one no one sense will dominate, though we may be tempted to read without letting any of the senses find a place.

Two things are to be remembered. *First,* choose a short incident, a single incident, in the life of Jesus. The above example is almost a violation of this, for it combines the return of the apostles from their first visitation with the feeding of the five thousand. Yet the two really belong together. To understand the second half, the first half is necessary, showing why Jesus was off in a desert spot away from the village stores. So choose a single incident, and meditate on it.

Second, take each one of the five senses as dominant in each of the five readings of the incident, not leaving out a single one, bringing into the meditation all the uncomfortable touches, the smelly scenes that are disagreeable, the pain and horror of the sick, the anger of the enemies in the later months of Jesus' life. To read each incident five times at least, studying a sense in each one, will create an understanding and a sympathy that will help one to live again with Jesus.

Then to close the meditation thank God in brief prayer for the insight that has come into the life and spirit of our own day through the life and spirit of Jesus in his own day. Finally, do what God may tell you to do as a result of this meditation.

14

The Fourteenth Week

THE MEDITATION

The old year has come to an end, and marvelous have been the blessings that have come to me. If Thou hadst given me insight to see ahead, I might not have chosen all Thou didst send. Yet if I had been doing all the choosing, I would have failed in bringing to myself some of the blessings that came. I would never have thought they might be mine!

I thank Thee, Father, that in Thy wisdom I have received all Thou didst send. Thou hast never given me too much to bear of trouble, though at times it seemed that I might break. In my own strength I found little help. But Thou didst strengthen me, that I might carry on.

Thou hast given me patience and understanding. Thou hast given me courage and faith. Thou hast given me persistence and endurance. But above all, Thou hast given me Thyself and Thy love. How can I return to Thee, in gratitude for what Thou hast given me, even a tiny portion of Thy love? Yet I would give myself to Thee.

I thank Thee for this new year, and humbly I offer Thee all that I have. My mind, my heart, my soul, my strength I give unto Thee. What it may bring I know not, but this one thing I know: that whereas I was blind, now I see! In that faith I turn to Thee, trusting that never once shall I be away from Thy love.

THE PAPER

MEDITATIONS ON THE LIFE OF JESUS

To be used with his meditations through the five senses, St. Ignatius of Loyola prepared a list of "mysteries" of Christ the

Lord as a basis for further meditation and contemplation. These largely follow Catholic principles, yet we may adapt them readily for Protestant usage.

Consider each of the following twelve "mysteries" in order, staying with each one until "it speaks to my condition." Read the scriptural passages for each, then reread them using the meditation of the five senses. After finding a new understanding of that phase in the life of Jesus, go on to the next "mystery." Begin the following day where you left off in the series the day before. Do not try to do all in one day, nor should any of them be hurried.

1. His Humble Birth—
   The Birth (Luke 2:1–20); His Growth (Luke 2:52); His Family (Mark 6:3)
2. Preparation—
   Temple Visit (Luke 2:31–49); Baptism (Matt. 3:13–17); Temptation (Luke 4:1–13)
3. Sermon on the Mount—
   The Beatitudes (Matt. 5:1–12); Fulfillment of the Law (Matt. 5:13–48)
4. The Healing Ministry—
   Peter's Mother-in-law (Mark 1:29–31); Multitudes Healed (Mark 1:32–45)
5. Prayer and Works—
   The Transfiguration (Mark 9:2–13); Healing a Lad (Mark 9:14–29)
6. The Passion Foretold—
   Peter's Confession (Mark 8:27–30); Suffering to Come (Mark 8:31–9:1)
7. March upon Jerusalem—
   Triumphal Entry (Luke 19:29–40); Cleansing the Temple (Matt. 21:12–17)
8. The Last Evening—
   The Supper (Matt. 26:20–35); Gethsemane (Matt. 26:36–46)
9. The Arrest—
   The Betrayal (Matt. 26:47–50); The High Priest (Matt. 26:57–68)
10. The Crucifixion—
    Before Pilate (Matt. 27:1–2, 11–26); The Cross (Matt. 27:32–44); The Death (Luke 23:39–49)

11. The Resurrection—
The Burial (Luke 23:50–56); The Resurrection (Mark 16:1–8);
(Luke 24:13–32)
12. The Testimony—
On Pentecost (Acts 2:1–4); Paul's Faith (I Cor. 15:1–11)

15

The Fifteenth Week

THE MEDITATION

I am a person full of many desires. Most of them are good, and
some of them are very good. But continually they conflict one with
another. I want to keep my health, yet I eat too much or too little,
and thus weaken myself. I wish to discipline my time, so as to be
more ready for service to Thee; yet I seek evenings of entertainment.
I would grow in the knowledge and love of Thy spirit, but I am
unwilling to sit down to careful thought and prayerful action.

Just what is it that I desire more than anything else? Is it that I
would find for myself friendships warm, beautiful, lovely? They are
a good thing, but is my life just to be the seeking of friendships for
myself? Or am I to give myself to Thee in devotion and loyalty that
will cause my acquaintances to turn from me?

Have I some secret desire, secret almost to myself, that I would
place first? Some desire to please me, to help me grow as I consider
my growth, to strengthen my devotion to Thee as I examine myself?
Or is it that I must give myself to Thee that Thou wilt create in
and through me something which I do not now understand?

Perhaps my desire is not for myself at all, but for someone whom
I love. Could it be that my desire is yet a selfish one, that through
them I may gain what I want, either for myself or for that one I
love? Help me to see myself as I really am, to know myself as Thou
dost know me!

More than anything else I would seek Thee. More than all else
I would serve Thee. Be with me, Eternal Spirit, that not my way
nor my will ever should come first in my life. Grant through Thy
loving wisdom that I may seek and find that which Thou wouldst
have me to do, have me to be, have me to say.

"Not my will, but thine be done."

THE PAPER

ON SIMPLICITY

We think too much about what others may say or think about
us and our actions. We do many things that fill our day largely
because we believe Society expects or demands that we do these
things. We would like to take time out for what we truly believe
are the important, significant actions of our living; but we are just
too busy with what everyone must admit is after all good. So we
tie ourselves in knots to serve in this or that, all of which we
believe are sincere acts of service for God. Yet Jesus said to busy
Martha: You are anxious about many things; Mary has chosen the
better way.

E. Herman in *Creative Prayer* writes:

When we read the lives of the saints, we are struck by a certain
large leisure which went hand in hand with a remarkable effectiveness.
They were never hurried. They did comparatively few things, and these
not necessarily striking or important; and they troubled very little about
their influence. Yet, they always seemed to hit the mark; every bit of
their life told. Their simplest actions had a distinction, an exquisiteness
which suggested the artist. The reason is not far to seek. Their saint-
hood lay in their habit of referring the smallest actions to God. They
lived in God. They acted from a pure motive of love towards God.
They were as free from self-regard as from slavery to the good opinion
of others. God's Son and God rewarded; what else needed they? Hence
the inalienable dignity of these meek, quiet figures that seem to produce such marvelous effects with such humble materials.[1]

Such simplicity comes out of abandonment of self in full commitment to God, a day-by-day renewal of commitment that says:

[1] Emily Herman: *Creative Prayer* (New York: Harper & Brothers, 1940),
p. 28.

Guide me this day, step by step, in all I do, *all*. When God becomes that Center of all our thinking, acting, feeling, it is as Thomas Kelly says in *Testament of Devotion*:

Life from the Center is a life of unhurried peace and power. It is simple. It is serene. It is amazing. It is triumphant. It is radiant. It takes no time, but it occupies all our time. And it makes our life programs new and overcoming. We need not get frantic. He is at the helm. And when our day is done we lie down quietly in peace, for all is well.[2]

This simplicity is in a twofold measure: First, it is simplicity in our faith, a complete trust in the love and providence of God as our Father that makes us say: I cannot get away from His love, for nothing I do is without Him. This has well been said by Fénelon two hundred years ago:

This liberty of a soul which sees immediately before it as it goes forward, but which loses no time reasoning about its steps, studying them, constantly considering those which it has already made, this is the true simplicity. . . . The more docile and yielding a soul is in letting itself be carried away without resistance or delay, the more it advances in simplicity. . . . The great obstacle to this happy simplicity is the foolish wisdom of the age, which wants to trust nothing to God, which wants to do everything by its own efforts, to arrange everything for itself, and to admire itself constantly in its works.[3]

Grou put it in similar words a century ago:

A simple heart will love all that is most precious on earth, husband or wife, parent or child, brother or friend in God, without marring its singleness: external things will have no attraction save inasmuch as they lead souls to Him; all exaggeration, unreality, affectation and falsehood must pass away from such an one, as the dews dry up before the sunshine. The single motive is to please God, and hence arises total indifference as to what others will say and think, so that words and actions are perfectly simple and natural, as in His Sight only. Such Christian simplicity is the very perfection of the interior life—God, His Will and pleasure its sole object.[4]

[2] Thomas Kelly: *op. cit.*, p. 124.
[3] François de Fénelon, *Christian Perfection* (New York: Harper & Brothers, 1947), pp. 195, 197, 198.
[4] Jean Grou, quoted in *The Choice Is Always Ours*, p. 399.

For today it may well be the simple conversation between a seeker and his God, in which we say: "What would You have me do in this affair? Speak to me with certainty that I may follow Your way. For I know Your love surrounds me." It is hearing God say in the depths of one's being: "Fear thou not; for I am with thee: be not dismayed; for I am thy God: I will strengthen thee; yea, I will help thee; yea, I will uphold thee with the right hand of my righteousness" (Isaiah 41:10); and then living one's life whole-heartedly in the light of that sentence.

But Christian simplicity has a second part too. Besides being simplicity in our faith and life, it is simplicity in choosing the concerns of our lfe. For the rush and pull of many appointments, all of which in the sight of man may well be wholly acceptable and fine, which create our distraction and anxiety and frayed nerves, are after all the result of our failure to achieve an inner wholeness. "The outer distractions," says Thomas Kelly, "of our interests reflect an inner lack of integration of our own lives." Fénelon said it without using these words of modern psychology and education when he wrote:

The great thing is to resign all your interests and pleasures and comfort and fame to God. He who unreservedly accepts whatever God may give him in this world—humiliation, trouble, and trial from within or from without—has made a great step towards self-victory; he will not dread praise or censure, he will not be sensitive; or if he finds himself wincing, he will deal so cavalierly with his sensitiveness that it will soon die away. Such full resignation and unfeigned acquiescence is true liberty, and hence arises perfect simplicity. Blessed indeed are they who are no longer their own, but have given themselves wholly to God.[5]

Let us then choose carefully in the light of our abandonment and our prayer what we should do, for it is not so much lack of time that hinders us as it is lack of that inner joy that is our very being.

This is the question, then, as posed by Thomas Kelly:

Do you *want* to live in such an amazing divine Presence that life is transformed and transfigured and transmuted into peace and power

[5] François de Fénelon, quoted in *The Choice Is Always Ours*, p. 23.

and glory and miracle? If you do, then you can. But if you say you haven't the time to go down into the recreating silences, I can only say to you, "Then you don't *really* want to, you don't love God above all else in the world, with all your heart and soul and mind and strength." For, except for spells of sickness in the family and when the children are small, when terrific pressure comes upon us, we find time for what we *really want* to do.

And he adds,

I find that a life of little whispered words of adoration, of praise, of prayer, of worship can be breathed all through the day. . . . There is a way of life so hid with Christ in God that in the midst of the day's business one is inwardly lifting brief prayers, short ejaculations of praise, subdued whispers of adoration and tender love to the Beyond that is within.[6]

16

The Sixteenth Week

The Meditation

On an old gate at Aberdeen University is the inscription, THEY SAY—WHAT DO THEY SAY? LET THEM SAY IT. Only maturity of mind and heart permits me to repeat that sentence! How can I forget what others may say about me?

Am I ashamed of my convictions? No, not at all! But Thou dost lead me into new ways that are so different from my former paths. I hesitate to change my life, because others will see how different I am! Will they think I am trying to be better than they are? Will they suspect I am "getting religion"? Is it, O Lord, that I am embarrassed to witness by a changed life the new way that is mine?

Whose approval do I seek? I desire friendships, and I cannot afford to lose a single one. I want to be loved. Yet I would turn

[6] Thomas Kelly, *op. cit.,* p. 120.

to Thee with all my heart, for Thy smile must come first. Help me, O Lord, to see first Thy kingdom, Thy love, Thy approval, even though others may not understand, even though they may criticize.

Grant to me, O God, the fullness of faith in Thee, of complete trust in Thy love. Teach me how to live before Thee and before my friends and loved ones that with assurance and loyalty I may reveal Thy love, Thy joy, Thy peace in every act, in every thought. I would put Thee first. I would not hesitate to witness for Thee. I do love Thee with my whole heart and soul and mind and strength.

"So they called the men in and ordered them not to speak or teach a single sentence about the Name of Jesus. But Peter and John replied: 'Decide for yourselves whether it is right before God to obey you rather than God; certainly we cannot give up speaking of what we have seen and heard.'" (Acts 4:18, 19, Moffatt.)

THE PAPER
RHYTHMIC BREATHING AND THE LORD'S PRAYER

In the practice of yogi Indians have discovered through the centuries the extreme importance of discipline over the body. By breath control, by muscular control, by appetite control, even by control of one's sleeping and awaking, spiritually-minded Indians have gone far in mental prayer and contemplation.

But such physical control of the body belongs to Christians too. Those who have gone apart in monastery or nunnery have opportunity for almost unlimited control over sleeping and eating, so that less and less sleep and smaller and smaller quantities of food and drink are necessary. Yet strangely enough, physical energy is quickened rather than lessened through such discipline.

For those of us who continue in an active life there is no desire for long hours of complete physical relaxation, nor is there time in our busy life for that. But we are learning that careful discipline of the body does permit far more activity with far less fatigue than we have known before. Going apart each day for an hour of quiet in solitude, with frequent intervals of a minute, more or less, a dozen times a day, we learn that renewal is almost instantaneous, renewal of physical energy as well as of mental and spiritual sensitivity.

Rhythmic breathing is an exercise used in many faiths through the years. For our purposes it has real value in slowing the tempo of our day without decreasing its activity. The plan is this:

First, either in one's quiet place, where he may sit still, or as one waits in room or store or for transportation, or while one is walking along or riding, offer a brief preparatory prayer, such as the following: "Bless Thou, O God, the regularity of my life, that Thou wilt be my Habit."

Second, with eyes open or closed, according to where one may be, begin saying the words of the Lord's Prayer, one word to each breath, doing this silently. Say only one word, then think of that word as long as the breath is held, going on to the next word with the next breath. Do not consciously hold the breath so as to prolong the intervals, but let such slowing down become gradual. Continue with each separate word of the entire Lord's Prayer, considering each as though rolling a tasty morsel upon the tongue.

Third, continue such an exercise until the breathing becomes slow and regular, a rhythm of patience and dignity, without the jerking and haste of un-Christian or ungentlemanly behavior.

Three things are to be kept in mind. One, the rhythmic breathing of this exercise is psychologically an excellent technique for relaxation, but a controlled relaxation, and one with purpose.

Second, after doing this several times with the Lord's Prayer, use the Twenty-third Psalm, the Beatitudes, the Communion Collect, or another such brief prayer or Scripture.

Third, if one desires to lengthen the time of this exercise, especially when alone in his quiet place, or when forced to wait someplace for an extended period, add to the Lord's Prayer other prayers or Scripture passages. But keep the perfect rhythm throughout of breathing and meditation.

17

The Seventeenth Week

THE MEDITATION

Thou art continually surprising me with the blessings Thou dost give unto me. I hardly turn around and Thou dost give me something new. How true it is that my world is one in which incredible things are happing—and fast!

More than all else Thou dost give me Thyself, a wonderful sense of Thy nearness and Thy love. Neither in the morning with the freshness of opportunity nor in the evening with the fatigue of a full day art Thou far from me. In times of quiet when I seek through recollection to draw myself to Thee, and in times of busyness when with others I share my love for Thee, Thou art with me.

Yet how new and how different are the revelations of Thy presence. A stranger passing by becomes a friend unseen, to be remembered because of Thy spirit through him touching me. A book casually picked from the table opens to me new doors into Thy holy temple. An experience, sometimes bitter, sometimes sweet, overwhelms me for a moment, and afterward I find the fullness of Thy love coming out of it. I stand amazed before the wonder and the mystery of Thy love for me.

> The Lord is my shepherd; I shall not want;
> Beside refreshing waters he leads me.
> He gives me new life;
> He guides me in paths of righteousness for His name's sake.
> Even though I walk in the darkest valley,
> I fear no harm; for Thou art with me.[1]

[1] *The Complete Bible, An American Translation* (Chicago: University of Chicago Press, 1939).

The Paper

MEDITATIONS ON PHRASES OF THE LORD'S PRAYER

(This series of spiritual exercises is based on practices not only for beginners, but for those also who are far along the way. At first glance, these exercises may seem kindergarten play, for they require joint action of mind and body in the same manner that a child learns to walk. Yet after a time a child moves his body either in walking or running without noticing each movement of hands or feet. His mind is then set free to observe where he may be going and why. So it is with these exercises. In their beginnings we must watch each step, until finally the habit fixes itself. Then through the exercise we indeed come into the presence of the Holy One.)

Finding a quiet place where one may sit or kneel in meditation, as one may desire, offer a preparatory prayer, such as: "Grant, O God, Thy blessing upon my intention, that through the words of my Master's prayer Thou wilt reveal Thyself to my mind and heart."

With eyes shut, or with them fixed upon one spot or object, so as to avoid distractions from wandering, repeat the first phrase of the Lord's Prayer, "Our Father." Think on this phrase, the word "Our" with all its meaning, and the word "Father" with all its fullness; and finally on the two together "Our Father." Stay with this phrase as long as there are further meanings, further insights, that come to the mind; as long as there arise additional longings, affections, delights that come to the heart. Do like the honey bee, which, St. Francis de Sales observes, dips deeper and deeper into the flower until all the nectar has been sipped, before it seeks another flowers.

Then take the second phrase, continuing the same considerations of mind and heart. Let each phrase become a part of one's consciousness until it enters one's inner being. Move on to each phrase of the prayer in its proper order until all have been considered.

St. Ignatius offers three rules to observe in connection with such an exercise. First, continue in this meditation on the phrases of the Lord's Prayer for one hour, but no more. It is well at the close of the meditation to repeat slowly the entire prayer, either mentally or orally.

Second, if in practicing this meditation one finds much for thought and affection in a single phrase or two, so that the hour draws to a close, do not hurry to others so as to complete the entire prayer. Stay with that phrase just as long as God speaks through it. But at the end of the hour, repeat the remainder of the prayer slowly. On the next day the exercise may be continued.

Third, if one has not completed as yet the entire prayer, repeat slowly the first phrases that have been considered, then dwell at length on the new phrase. Again, if the hour draws to a close before the full prayer is completed, repeat these remaining phrases slowly.

At the end of each day's meditation, after repeating slowly the Lord's Prayer, offer a brief prayer of consecration, such as: "Accept my gratitude, Lord God, for the thoughts and affections that have come from Thee in this hour; and bless to Thy service the resolves that I bring unto Thee."

Many have found it helpful to keep a notebook at hand, in which they may enter thoughts and resolves that arise during the meditation. They are jotted down quickly during the course of the meditation and expanded afterward, for it is better not to interrupt the hour.

18

The Eighteenth Week

THE MEDITATION

A third of my life is spent in sleep, a requirement of my physical being. I need a silent body and a silent mind in order to be refreshed for the next day's activity.

One day in seven I am granted a time of refreshment and change, because men have found through the years that growth will be stunted unless this day of rest is used. So it is that during the course of the year I am granted further vacation, change from school, from work, so that in variety of activity I may further refresh myself.

Silence has been found to be one of the finest instruments by which I may grow, mentally as well as spiritually, and even in a physical sense. What a relief it is to get away from a noisy spot so as to rest my ears! No wonder I begin to shout at the top of my voice even when I am in a quiet spot. I had to do it in the noise!

Now in the silence I can begin to straighten out some of my thinking. Who am I? Where did I come from? Where am I going? What am I? These are not answered quickly, but only the fool refuses to ask them, or refuses to seek for answers. I am on the way to maturity, and maturity of mind and spirit demands such answers.

So let me ask myself: What am I doing in return for the gift of life? How am I filling a place that would be empty without me? Where can I share the good things that God has given me, in school, in play, in church, in work, at home?

Father, I thank Thee for these my friends, and that with them in the silence, in the praise of hymn and Scripture, in class work and in play, I may find Thy love.

THE PAPER

MEDITATION ON THE WILL OF GOD

St. Francis de Sales offered many exercises for meditation in his *Introduction to a Devout Life,* some of which are hardly usable in Protestant practice. Others can be taken over almost in detail, and many can be readily adapted for modern Protestant usage. One of these last concerns the will of God.

Finest of all prayers to make our own is that of Jesus: "Not my will but Thine be done." How to find for ourselves that will is the difficult matter. Gerald Heard says:

He, then, who would be guided, will always be in a state of readiness to listen to questions (from God), and also in a state of humility to know that not till many years will he be able to answer. . . . When the soul has reached such readiness and openness that it is prepared to realize that there is no chance or accident, then in every circumstance large and small, and in every split second it can hear the voice of God asking it whether it wishes to do His will.[1]

To help find over the years an increasing understanding of the will of God, practice this exercise.

First, consider while we walk along or as we sit in quiet, the *general will* of God, by which as Creator of the universe He wills all His works upon earth and in the earth. Consider how rain falls on the just and the unjust, the sun shines upon the good and the evil. The beauty and majesty of His handiwork is freely given for all to see and have. The Eternal God generously gives to all mankind the earth upon which we live. Then offer prayers of approval, of praise, of thanksgiving, of adoration for His love, His holiness, His beauty, His justice.

Second, consider next the *special will* of God, by which He loves His own, and in which He reveals His providential care. Consider the comfort and assurance that come through His strength granted us, and the sorrow that yet falls upon us, by which we grow into true spiritual maturity. Think more deeply and understandingly of the troubles that often befall good folk, yet, offer again prayers of approval, of praise, of thanksgiving and of adoration.

Third, consider then the *personal will* of God as it touches yourself, in all the good and evil that happen to your own person. Try to see beneath the surface of outward events to the underlying Hand of God by which you are sustained. Then offer prayers of approval, of praise, of thanksgiving, of adoration.

Fourth, complete the meditation with *an act of confidence* in the will of God, that even though you may not know what is to come, it will work all good for you and your happiness.

Then St. Francis adds: "When you have performed this exercise two or three times in this way, you can shorten it, vary it and arrange it, as you find best, for it should often be thrust into your heart as an aspiration."

[1] Gerald Heard: *Prays and Meditations* (New York: Harper & Brothers, 1949), p. 44.

19

The Nineteenth Week

THE MEDITATION

Thanks be to Thee, O God, who giveth us the victory through our Lord Jesus Christ.

Victory over myself, my weakness, my pride, my sense of inferiority, my belief in my importance. Thou hast helped me to see myself in relationship to Thee and to others. I cannot claim from Thee by my own merits any good thing. But Thou hast given me a multitude of blessings, and above them all is the gift of Thy Spirit by which I have become a whole person. The unbroken circle of my life is a gift from Thee.

Victory over outward circumstances, sickness and pain and suffering and freedom from any hurt of the body, poverty of possessions or an abundance of material things, and from the heritage that is mine and the environment into which I have been placed. Thou hast helped me to see that kicking against fate is useless, that using to the full what Thou dost give me alone brings blessing. Thou hast shown me ways to serve in spite of limitations of my own or of my environment. Thou hast taught me the way of inner resources by which to stand in time of outward disaster or plenitude. I am not an animal beat upon by the club of circumstance, but I am a child of Thy spirit, able to rise above any beatings of life.

Yet in myself and my own efforts there is no victory at all. I stand helplessly before Thee. But through the gift of Thy spirit I find the promise true: Thy grace is sufficient for me. Temper the wind to me as Thou dost temper the wind to the shorn lamb. For I would love Thee with the fullness of my love. I can find no rest except as I find my rest in Thee.

The Paper

WE RETURN TO COMMITMENT

Once again we come back to the thought of commitment. It is necessary to our growth that we should return to it.

Commitment is giving oneself in complete trust to the love and will of God. It is not accepting a belief, not even belief in God or in Christ. That is wholly an intellectual assent to some proposition made by another. But it is giving one's whole life, completely and utterly, in simple trust, to the God of our belief.

So the beginning of commitment is in choosing the One to whom we will entrust our whole being. For the Christian it is the Father God to whom Jesus gave himself. He is the God of love, who watches over us so that even a sparrow does not fall without the Father seeing. Though He is the Creator of the ends of the earth, and though He is the Judge before Whom we rise and fall, He is yet the Eternal Spirit of Love, to Whom we may pray "Our Father."

Then accepting the God and Father of Jesus as our God and our Father, we give all we have to Him, trusting that His love and care will surround us continually. What has happened to us we believe has been not without His knowledge. What will happen to us we believe will be only in His love. So shall we be unafraid of what may come, for we are completely and wholly obedient to Him, Who loves us with deep love.

But this is a continuing commitment, not started and ended by a single act. As Olive Wyon says: "To give ourselves thus to Him, to let Him mould and train us and use us as He wills, is not the work of a day but of a lifetime; it is not accomplished in a single act of surrender, but it is an attitude of heroic choice and acceptance, endlessly renewed." [1] Each day we pray anew, "Thy kingdom come, thy will be done." There must be persistence in this, no turning back from this complete trust in God's love and mercy. As we progress day by day, we shall find it more simple to trust, for we shall know with growing certainty that we are becom-

[1] Olive Wyon: *The School of Prayer* (Philadelphia, Westminster Press, 1944), p. 42.

ing one with Him. That is why Miss Wyon also could write: "As we follow this path there will grow upon us the sense that we are 'in the way'; we shall come to know, very quietly, by a kind of 'inner awareness' whether we are to turn to the right hand or to the left, or whether we are to keep straight on. Peace will be ours, for there can be no anxiety for those who have handed over the direction of their lives to God." [2]

There is no such anxiety or fear because we know nothing will be too much for us. We are no longer ourselves, for we are His. Hence, what He asks us to do we can do, for He will both guide us in doing it and grant us the strength for the doing. That is where our morning prayer each day will have its special place, as Fénelon suggests: "A look of confidence, a simple turning of your heart to him will renew you, and although you often feel dull and discouraged, yet every moment during which God asks you to do something, he will give you the ability and the courage according to your need. This is the daily bread which we ask for hourly and which will never fail us." [3]

Through listening to Him, through searching for His will for each one of us, we will step forth gladly into each new day, knowing that mistakes will be made because of our human imperfection and our failure to eliminate self completely. But we will press on as those forgiven, certain that our intent is to do His will, and that He will bless that intent. "Thou wilt keep him in perfect peace, whose mind is stayed on thee." (Isaiah 26:3)

(For those who may wish further study, read the chapter on "Holy Obedience" in *A Testament of Devotion* by Thomas Kelly. Also read from *The Choice Is Always Ours* as follows: pages 26–28, 434–436 (the last two paragraphs especially), 32–35, 40–44, 21–23).

[2] Olive Wyon, *ibid.*, p. 46.
[3] François de Fénelon, *op. cit.*, p. 12.

20

The Twentieth Week

THE MEDITATION

What I could do with a large income if I had it! I'd help so many folk who are in need. As it is, I have just enough to get along in my social class, and after my family and my interests are cared for, if any is left, I'd gladly give it to the Red Cross or to the church or some other worthy project. Or would I? Am I really excusing my stinginess by calling attention to the little I have? Am I covering up my selfishness by revealing loudly the little I do give?

Thou knowest I love Thee and would serve Thee. If I were free to go here and go there, I would gladly do so. But I just don't have time. After I take care of my business duties or household needs, I must find a little recreation with my friends. As soon as my family grows up or my business details lessen, then I will take time to work in church or community activities. Or will I? If I don't take a little time when I have only a little, will I take more time when I have that?

When I really know that my faith is strong and that my life is good, I am going to give part of my life to Thee through the church, by serving in some of its less "showy" places, by calling on neighbors who have moved near me, by talking to folk about their religious life. But I am not ready yet, not having found for myself all the answers. Someday I will truly be a missionary in my own community. Or will I? If I don't share what I now have found, if I can't serve because I haven't as yet learned all the answers, will I ever be able to do so?

Am I truly sincere in my Christian practice, or is it a camouflage for emptiness, emptiness of heart and soul? God, help me to see the truth!

THE PAPER

COMMITMENT OF ONE'S MONEY

No commitment is complete that leaves out any portion of one's life or thought. We must offer ALL of ourselves, or we are one of Thomas Kelly's "half-committed" men. Strength and joy and peace, in the long last, are for those who are totally committed. That means commitment of one's mind, one's heart, one's body, one's time and even one's money.

In the Old Testament days—and the same is quite true for other religions besides that of our Hebrew forefathers—the tithe was one's gift to the Eternal Spirit. This tithe was the "firstfruits" (in the early agricultural days) of crops and animals, even at times including the first-born son, as was mentioned briefly in the Paper for the Twelfth Week. (Hannah presented Samuel, her first-born son, to the temple, to be trained as a priest. Joseph and Mary much later presented Jesus as a special offering, in a somewhat different sense, as their first-born son.) This meant giving the very best to God, not waiting for the smaller and second-rate pickings which would mean a lower price on the market or a lower quality of goods.

Tithing as practiced in these days means proportionate giving, a certain percentage of one's income being set aside upon receiving that income, this sum to be used for charitable purposes, not only for the Church itself. For some this is 5 per cent of the income, for others the Biblical 10 per cent, while others, having even larger incomes, make the percentage much higher.

Normally also it is based on one's net income. That means a businessman may or may not take out first the necessary expenses of his work. Others remove "deductions" first, or base their tithe only upon take-home pay; though no one who tithes deducts personal expenses at all. The point is: in our free fellowship, men decide as individuals of free choice just how this will be done.

But underlying every bit of tithing is complete confidence and trust in the goodness and mercy of God, in which the tither believes that if he first gives his tithe, then he will find it possible to live on the remainder. But how can I know? someone asks. We cannot know one single thing about the future with complete certainty. We say: I believe in God's care, and I am willing to experiment in commitment, even with my money. If God does not honor my faith, and I find that after a period of three months or longer I just cannot make ends meet, then I will no longer give Him His share until I have made certain of my share. It is an adventure in faith to which the Christian agrees, believing that God, if not prospering him, will at least give him what he needs. No one accepting this commitment has kept it faithfully and then has found God faithless. Yet we do not bargain with Him at all. We say: "These first fruits belong to God. I give them to Him. He will help me to live on what is left."

Then there is even more to consider. What of the remainder of our money, after the tithe has been taken out? What is to happen to that?

One committed to God will not spend one penny more upon himself than he needs, nor will he waste one single penny in any way. He will not be stingy. He will be creative. He will be more careful of his personal expenses. He will simplify his living. His entire income, in other words, will be committed to God.

Again, no man can tell another exactly what to do with each dollar of his income. Some must listen to Jesus as he speaks to the young ruler who was told to sell all, then follow Jesus. For most of us prayer and meditation in the quiet hour will open up Christian ways to use our money. Then we will know that one specific portion is set aside directly as a tithe for the Lord's work; while all the rest equally is the Lord's too. We will indeed be stewards of the Eternal God.

21

The Twenty-first Week

THE MEDITATION

A writer has said that a person's character is marked not so much by what life does to him as to the reaction he makes to life's circumstances.

Yes, but I have been handicapped through no fault of my own. A physical disability is nothing to pass by simply. Whether I like it or not, I am limited in certain activities because of that disability. More, I have not had the opportunities of leisurely living that come to those with financial stability. Hence, I could not take time to read, to study, to travel, to cultivate the beginnings of artistic ability, which leisure permits. I have had to be busy with mundane pursuits, just to exist!

Yet, come to think about it, my reaction to these things is the important fact! Either I could bewail my fate, such a pleasant thing to do to excuse my lack of gumption, and thus place the blame on life itself; or I could take my life up into my hands and make of it what it could be under the circumstances. After all, it is in my power, and in no one else's power, what I do with my life.

Forgive me, O merciful God, that time and time again I have been bitter because of the so-called evils that life has hurled at me, the "evils" of poor health, of meager income, of across-the-tracks residence, of few opportunities to reveal to others the high abilities I knew I had! I have tried to escape by putting the blame upon circumstance, by making someone else bear the fault, by arguing with myself that if I had a chance, then what couldn't I do!

I thank Thee that Thou hast helped me to avoid bitterness and jealousy and hopelessness and defeat. I have had to bow my head, but with Thy help I have never had to surrender, except to Thee. Grant me Thy courage all the days and years of my life.

THE PAPER

COMMITMENT OF ONE'S TIME

Each one of us has exactly the same amount of time. Some have responsibilities of children, of daily work, of care for others, that take away from one's leisure. But each one has the same twenty-four hours.

It is equally obvious that we can always add to what we are now doing, even if our time is closely scheduled, by eliminating first some present activity. It is a matter of choice. If we are busy with one organization, and seek to join another, we must first drop part of that first activity, or eliminate something else, before we shall find that extra time we seek.

The choice is not always ours. Sometimes health forbids our entrance upon certain things, even cutting down the amount of time we may spend gainfully. Sometimes the care of an elderly person almost completely forbids our acceptance of duties and pleasures we may otherwise have. The constant care of a small child obviously does not permit free use of our time.

Yet with all the duties that as Christians we must assume, at home, at school, at work, in community sharing, we do have certain free time. This must be used for extra rest and sleep often enough, and frequently it must be used for some form of recreation, so that we shall not break under the nervous tension of our day. In this same leisure time comes most of our church and community service, as well as our own personal devotional growth. How we use it will depend upon the degree of our commitment.

For one thing, we need to plan our day, just as a teacher plans her classwork, or an executive plans his office routine. If we know ahead of time that at a certain hour we need to meet a specific appointment, we will plan toward it. So with the normal routine of household tasks, of committee responsibilities, of finding time for quiet and meditation, it is merely bringing order out of chaos. Nearly every cause for tardiness rests upon chaotic living, no orderliness in little things. In the early morning write down, if need be, the major tasks for the day; then cross them off the list. If some can wait until the morrow, let them do so, particularly if a new task that must be faced immediately arises. By putting first things first, there will always be time to get these that are truly important completed.

Olive Wyon comments: "Another source of difficulty in prayer is *spiritual carelessness*: wasting time; the habit of 'putting off' till tomorrow what should have been done today; failure to *plan* our time, so that hurry creeps in, and 'hurry is the death of prayer.'" [1]

To avoid a sense of hurry, though there must be urgency in all we do as Christians, we must leave gaps of time in our scheduled plans, either so that we may face emergencies that will arise, or so as to make certain we are not hurried by the ticking clock. Some things always can wait if necessary, and that leads to the next thought.

Second, we need to choose wisely those things which are truly important. Here is where many raise the question: With so much to do, how can I find time for quiet and prayer? Betty White, quoted in *Letters of the Scattered Brotherhood*, asks: "Have you anything more important to do? Ask yourself that question when interruptions threaten and you are tempted to set this hour aside." One must consider the reasons behind our doing what we do. How much is done because we seek the approval of others? We feel we must "keep up with the Joneses" in a nonfinancial way! Or how much do we do ineffectively, because we scatter our energy with many things, instead of concentrating it upon one thing? It is better to know something in general about social and economic and racial problems, but to give our specific attention and study to just one of them, and then perhaps in only one phase at that. Otherwise we become a jack of all trades, and indeed a master of none.

Third, it is up to us and no one else what we do with our free time. Over that we do have complete control. With it we can make time for personal religious growth. Again Olive Wyon comes directly to the point:

To find this space and solitude, however, usually means that we have got to *make* it. We have to think out our way of living, and plan to get the amount of time to ourselves that we need. Even people

[1] Olive Wyon, *op. cit.*, p. 88.

who think they "have no time" would find that they usually have time for the things they most want to do. Even those who have the most exacting work, and whose time is claimed by others almost continually, could find brief spaces for "recollection" if they knew what to do. I think it is ignorance of the use of time for prayer and thought that is the real hindrance, not the lack of time itself. Even the most over-burdened people would find their work less heavy if they were in the habit of taking brief draughts of "living water." God is *there* all the time; a silent glance, a brief prayer uttered from the heart in the midst of the din of factory or a kitchen is as dear to Him as the prayer of those who have more leisure.[2]

Finally, and the hint of this is in Miss Wyon's comment, we need not find great blocks of time. We do have many small bits of it, which we waste in idleness. Carry a pocket book of devotions, and when waiting for the bus, for the coming of a friend, for the doctor's appointment, read a page or two as time permits. Or frequently through the day, between tasks at home, in the shift of classes at school, at odd moments that are ever ours, lift a prayer to God for yourself, for another, of thanksgiving, of petition, of intercession.

Commitment is no idle matter. It is the utter giving of ourselves to the Eternal God, in the midst of where we are, with what we have. Time is what we all have, some in larger degree than others, but it is invaluable. We can keep it for ourselves, but the committed person gives it all to God. As a result, such a person finds he can do far more with less tiredness than ever before. For God is his partner.

For further reading:

Bro, *More Than We Are*, Chapter 4, "Time To Pray."
Wyon, *The School of Prayer*, chapter on "Prayer and Life," pp. 59–69.
Kelly, *A Testament of Devotion*, section on "Simplicity," p. 63 ff.
Phillips, *The Choice Is Always Ours*, as follows:
"The Habitual Cast of Thought," two sections, pp. 132–133.
"Necessity for Habitual Prayer," pp. 294–295.
"The Element of Time," p. 228.

[2] Olive Wyon, *ibid.*, p. 60.

Chapter Eight on "Action," especially pp. 354–355, 356–357, 360, 363, 363–365.
"Three Levels of Action," pp. 434–436.

22

The Twenty-second Week

The Meditation

Speak, Lord, for thy servant heareth! My ears are often dull, and my eyes so oft are dim; yet I would that Thou shouldst come unto me. Make me aware of Thy spirit!

Thou hast spoken to me in the beauty of the fall season, in the wide expanse of the winter's snow, the budding of the springtime, the fullness of summer's heat; Thou art the Creator of all life, and I have heard Thy voice above Thy creation.

Thou hast spoken to me in the humble prayers of a devout father, in the quiet encouragement of a loving mother, in the sympathy and wise understanding of good teachers, in the deep love and affection of knowing friends. How thankful I am unto Thee, O God, for those surrounding me who have spoken by word and deed of Thee.

Thou hast spoken to me in the simple events of my common day, helping me to be patient in my disappointments, humble in my achievements, grateful for Thy discipline. In my few moments of true joy I have heard Thee, and in the waves of sorrow I have been upheld by Thy strength. In the busyness of my day and in its leisure, Thou hast spoken to me. In the fullness of my devotion to Thee, and in the emptiness of my turning from Thee, still hast Thou visited me.

Not for ecstasy and fervor do I pray, but for the steady, certain assurance of Thy continued touch upon my life. For this, O God, is my life.

The Paper

ON BEING "USED" BY GOD

In our praying we offer ourselves to God, saying, "I give myself to Thee; take me; use me." What do we mean?

First, we mean there is One Whose love we may trust, to Whom we can offer ourselves. God is our Father, seeking us in love. We must be certain of this, else we cannot offer ourselves to Him. If He is far off and too busy to be bothered with us, or if He is only the Creator God, no longer having any concern for us individually now that He has started the long chain of creation, then we cannot and will not "give" ourselves to such an impersonal or uninterested Force.

We must begin by believing God is interested in each one of us, and by living in accordance with that belief. When we do so turn to Him with complete confidence and trust in His love and providence, we are then ready to make the perfect sacrifice, the sacrifice of our very lives to Him in uttter commitment. Then we say: "We are finite; we know not what today, and much less tomorrow, will bring. Nevertheless, we give ourselves to Thee, to serve Thee. Use us as Thou wilt."

Only as we offer ourselves freely and gladly to Him in this way, without demanding of Him immediate insight into a particular deed by which He may "use" us, can we truly be ready to be "used" in the specific task that presents itself. Without reservation, without qualification, without holding back a single portion of mind and heart and body, we must present ourselves "a living sacrifice, holy, acceptable to God." If we must know first where and how He is to use us, then we have not committed ourselves. Like soldiers enlisting in warfare, we must engage ourselves to go and to do all our commanding officer orders.

But we can know His will specifically when we have so committed ourselves, as we face each moment of the day. Rising in the morning I may ask: "Use me to speak for Thee words of comfort, of cheer, of encouragement to those I meet this morning. In each task of my day, speak through me, act through me, that Thy love, Thy kindliness, Thy strength may enter those I meet."

He will then use us as channels for comfort, for wisdom, for judgment, for courage, for joy, for patience, none of which is our own, but each of which comes from Him. We will find that such a prayer before attempting every single task will open opportunities by which we may soon know He indeed is using us.

Be like a child; look at thy two feet and say, Lord, walk these for me. Talk to him as to thy friend and nurse. Be in sweet common friendship with him. Call him in thy bath, in thy daily tasks, in thy going from one room to another. Say, Nay, I will not go alone. Come, be thou with me, lead thou the way. Behold, he will answer then, and come running like laughter and golden hope into thy heart, and with understanding love will he walk with thee from room to room. And too, will he stand beside thee when thou faceth thy friends and visitors, and he will place a hand in thine and will watch thy heart and the issues therefrom so that thou canst talk in perfect safety knowing that thy words will be food and drink and life to all in thy presence.

For thou hast him all to thyself. He is thine—forever. Do not puzzle how he can see thy two feet when there are millions of feet, that is too much for thy understanding. Enough that it is the truth that he hath never failed to come when called and that he will come as thou dost want him.[1]

Read Matthew 25:31–46; Isaiah 6:1–13.

23

The Twenty-third Week

THE MEDITATION

A young woman said she wanted to climb the ladder of humility. Her director told her: "Begin by seeing how often you can accept correction without excuse."

But how difficult that is! Thou knowest how weak I am, Father.

[1] *Letters of the Scattered Brotherhood,* ed. by Mary Strong (New York: Harper & Brothers, 1948), pp. 31-32.

I make frightful mistakes. I would that Thou shouldst teach me true humility, that I may see myself as I really am, that I may have no exalted sense of my own importance.

Yet whenever I do something that is wrong, I do not want my wrong mentioned before others. Of course not! Though on second thought, part of the sharing of a group that loves each other is to point out where I am wrong. Help me to accept such correction when it is in love, even though I may not see the good in it at the time.

I know I do resent criticism and correction. I am an adult, and I think carefully before most of my actions. And I know that the one who corrects me does not always do what is the right thing. He should think of his own wrongdoing before he tells me about mine! I just don't like to be told off, even when kindly and lovingly done.

Yet I must accept such correction without alibi, even when it is seemingly unjust. I must not begin to point out the weaknesses of my accuser. I must not begin to qualify my own weakness. I must not irritably call attention to similar weaknesses in others whom the accuser does not happen to mention. I am like Peter, who asked Jesus: "What of him?" pointing toward John.

Forgive me, O God, for my tendency to answer back, to alibi, to excuse myself. I do make mistakes, I am careless, I am thoughtless, I am unforgiving. I act as though I never required correction. Forgive my selfishness, O God. I would truly love Thee.

THE PAPER

FAITH IN ACTION

Out of football comes this remarkably pointed illustration by Steve Owens, coach of the New York Giants professional football team: "It's not what you do in the huddle that counts. It's what you do when you come out of it."

Like all such illustrations it is slightly exaggerated, for Owens knows that in the huddle is the place for decision as to what the team should do. But no games are won there. Too long there means a penalty. Games are won when the team comes out of the huddle and goes into action.

So with the Christian life. We need the "prayer huddle," for without it we would miss a sense of direction, of purpose, of decision. But Jesus said that the way we reveal our love for God found in quiet is through love for man in daily life. For Him the test of our faith is what we do about it in daily living.

1. Criticism of others disappears. Our critical attitude of tearing apart our friends and enemies, of objecting to their inefficiencies or their weaknesses, of asking how "they get that way," suddenly disappears. We not only find that we have lost this common trait, but hearing folk attack others critically disturbs us.

2. Everyone seems so friendly. Beneath the worry and anxiety of our living we sense the open faces and smiling hearts of people. Our smiles in return bring a warmth and a joy that fill our whole being.

3. We reach out with love to all we meet, even the strangers we have not seen before. We want to help everyone, to make certain they too are happy. Just ordinary kindnesses begin to multiply, and we find that normal courtesies and thoughtful deeds are part of everyday living. We have no desire to help only those who can help us; we just want to help folk, any folk, who need what we have or can offer.

4. We seek little common tasks in church and community. These once seemed so puny, things hardly worth our time. Now we want to help make drapes, to work at a supper, to teach a class, to do some typing, to clean a room, to paint a chair, to visit in a shutin's home. Just to be doing something for the church or community is really doing something for God—how joyous is that feeling!

5. Our money begins to assume new significance. We need less and less for ourselves, and we want to give more and more for others. We lose interest in extra clothing and extra desserts and midday snacks and luxuries that we thought quite necessary. We seek ways of saving from our regular allowances, as well as cutting down on our regular expenditures, that we may have gifts to share with others.

6. We rearrange our time. We spend less time in beauty parlors, in movies, in other forms of commercial recreation, in seeking pleasure for ourselves alone. We begin to drop out of some organi-

zations and committees through which we have been scattering our energies, that we may give more time to fewer things, yet truly give enough time to these to make our work effective. We begin putting first things first, surprising ourselves by the amount of time we have and the amount of work we now can do. In office and in home and in school we are amazed as we wonder why we never had worked out such a fine time schedule before.

7. We find that our minds reach out far beyond their former horizons. We no longer are provincial, thinking of self, of immediate family, of immediate neighborhood. We seek books, friends, classes, entertainment that will enlarge our minds and our thinking. We begin to read and talk and think about social problems, about race and industry and government. Good housing and juvenile delinquency and correct voting and care for the needy and the general welfare of those in any need begin to be part of our living. We seek to bring God's kingdom where we live.

24

The Twenty-fourth Week

THE MEDITATION

Elijah, running away from Mount Carmel after the test of fire and the destruction of the prophets of Baal, went into hiding in the desert. There God came to him and Elijah complained, "I, only I, am left!" But God answered, "Seven thousand are in Israel, the knees of which have not bowed to Baal." [I Kings 18, 19.]

I thank Thee for the fellowship of those concerned with me in knowing and doing Thy will. At times it has been a difficult discipline to examine myself in the light of Thy judgment and Thy love, but these my friends have given me encouragement and hope. When in my inner thoughts I have seemed farthest from Thee, and most alone, I have found my strength through this fellowship.

Help me to see, O God, that I do not stand alone in all my experiences of life. Teach me to understand that as a human being I do make mistakes, I do need Thy forgiveness, I do receive Thy compassionate love. Forgive me for my complaining when I cannot see as far as I wish to see. Grant me patience to wait in Thy love, to rest in Thy care.

Thou hast blessed me through my friends who share with me my search for Thy will. Their love, their patience, their insight, their assurance, their understanding have opened my eyes to Thy Spirit. Accept Thou my gratitude for what they have shared with me, and bless to them the little which I have been permitted to share with them.

But above all, O Thou Eternal One, I thank Thee for Thyself, for Thy continuing presence with me, for Thy leading of my spirit, for Thy provident care over me, for the fullness of Thy love so graciously poured out upon me. I would merit Thy love by the gift of my life to Thee. Accept what I have to offer Thee, and bless to Thy service my love, my joy, my peace, my faith.

"Bless the Lord, O my soul, and all that is within me, bless His holy name."

THE PAPER

ASPIRATIONS AND WATCHWORDS

Throughout the Bible there are thousands of passages, aspirations, promises, "faithful sayings," which have become the watchwords or "particular property" of many individuals. It almost seems as though that one verse or so was written just for a certain person. Frequently folk choose such passages and gather them together to make their own "Bible," chapters and verses which become—sometimes with whole books—their special Bible.

For our purposes in these fellowship groups two kinds are of importance; first, those aspirations which repeated over and over again bring one into a sense of the immediate presence of God; and second, those promises which through the years have been proven valid by those repeating them, promises that become part of one's thought and action.

First, with these aspirations, choose one, and repeat it slowly and thoughtfully over and over, letting its adoration become yours. Repeat it several times during the quiet time, or a hundred times during the course of the day.

    a. My Lord and my God (John 20:28).

    b. Bless the Lord, O my soul: and all that is within me, bless His holy name. Bless the Lord, O my soul, and forget not all his benefits (Psalm 103:1).

    c. Whom have I in heaven but thee? and there is none upon earth that I desire beside thee? (Psalm 73:25).

    d. Even from everlasting to everlasting, thou art God (Psalm 90:2).

    e. As the hart panteth after the water brooks, so panteth my soul after thee, O God (Psalm 42:1).

Second, use these promises in your time of need, adding to them others to be found in your Bible reading.

    a. Fear thou not, for I am with thee: be not dismayed; for I am thy God: I will strengthen thee; yea, I will help thee; yea, I will uphold thee with the right hand of my righteousness (Isaiah 41:10).

    b. Come unto me, all ye that labour and are heavy laden, and I will give you rest (Matthew 11:28).

    c. The Lord is my light and my salvation; whom shall I fear? the Lord is the strength of my life; of whom shall I be afraid? (Psalm 27:1).

    d. In quietness and in confidence shall be your strength (Isaiah 30:15).

    e. Love never faileth (I Corinthians 13:8).

    f. With God all things are possible (Matthew 19:26).

    g. The Lord is my shepherd; I shall not want (Psalm 23:1).

    h. The Lord will deliver him in time of trouble (Psalm 41:1).

At times a Psalm—for a great many the Twenty-third Psalm— and at times a hymn will become a watchword, a source of strength and courage. Always these come out of one's experience rather un-

expectedly, written clearly within the mind as though etched there.
Hold fast to them when they come, for they are words of life.

25

The Twenty-fifth Week

THE MEDITATION

I thank Thee, Father, that I am an individual. I am different
from all other people, even though I am like all others. Thou hast
made me to have a mind of my own, a personality that I call myself.

But every time I get into trouble, it is because of me. My self
gets in my way, demanding MY share, MY rights, MY vengeance. I
am like a child refusing to play unless the play goes just as I
want it. After all, I must stand up for myself, or I will become
a nonentity. How can that be, when Thou hast given me that
by which I may be an individual?

Yet I am slowly learning the lesson that only as I can be rid of
self can I grow beyond my present level of spiritual life. I must
turn over my whole life to Thee, to Thy direction, to Thy com-
mand, to Thy will, if I am to become the one that I should be.
Then, and then only, as I lose my life in Thee can I truly save my
life.

Help me, my Father, to get rid of myself. Help me to give all
that I have to Thee, my mind, my heart, my body, my very soul.
Teach me to listen prayerfully to Thee, to Thy wisdom, to Thy
guidance, that day by day and every day I may grow farther and
farther away from my own desires and closer and closer to Thy
desires for me.

Draw me to Thee with Thy love. Open the door of my spirit
wider that Thy spirit may find room. Grant unto me that not my
will but Thine may be done.

THE PAPER

WHAT TO PRAY FOR

Even though we have been experimenting together for nearly six months, some of us still find it difficult to know what to pray for. Much prayer should be thanksgiving and praise, for the beginnings of a new day and for the work of the day as it comes to a close, for the untold blessings that touch us every hour, for the special mercies of an understanding Father. But frequent prayer will be petition for self and intercession for others.

1. For one's self—

Let our prayers always be for spiritual things, not physical. We rest upon the love and mercy of God, and place ourselves in His everlasting arms. We cannot always know His infinite will for us. For our own growth it may be best that hunger of body and spirit, sickness of mind and body, loneliness, times of financial strain, periods of confusion and doubt as to correct choices should touch us. Through our own pain of body and spirit we can be a source of strength to others in understanding love and sympathy.

But God always wants us to ask for the things of the Spirit, for His guidance in our choices, for His wisdom in our thinking, for His Love and Light and Radiance in all our day. These and many others can be ours regardless of health or wealth or any other thing. But without them health and wealth and work to do are empty things.

Let our prayer be like these:

Father, I am afraid. Remove my fear from me, and send in its place Thy courage. I see no solution for this that bothers me, but I will not fret. I hold it before Thee, knowing that in Thy wisdom and love nothing is too much for Thee. Now I lay hold of Thy love, and in Thee will I find my rest.

Take me this day, O God, and use me as Thou wilt. I do not choose the day, but I do choose Thee. May the Light of Thy spirit chase away the darkness of my soul. Let the music of Thy voice be a song in my heart.

In the midst of my sorrow and pain I cry unto Thee, O God. Break me if need be, but hide not Thy face from me. I ask for strength to endure, patience to wait, courage to persist.

2. For others—

a. Let our prayers always be positive, never negative. Send no thoughts into the mind of another through God that would darken his mind. Send only thoughts of love and radiance and peace and helpfulness that will brighten his mind through God.

Let our prayer be like these:

Father God, —— needs Thy love and peace. Quiet her restlessness, touch her heart with Thy hand of love, grant her the stillness of Thy peace.

I would remember ——. Warm his heart with the flow of Thy presence, and make bright his day. Let the healing touch of Thy spirit cool his fevered mind and harassed body. Hold him in the fullness of Thy love.

Bless Thou ——, and use her faithfulness, her loyalty, her devotion. Accept her witness of Thee, that she may know the joy of Thy words: Well done, thou good and faithful servant.

b. Let our prayers wait patiently for God to move in His way, not in ours. We will be tempted to "force" His hands, by praying, "Make him come to church" or "Tell her she should do this" or the like. These are negative, and insist upon OUR way. Instead, hold our friend before the love of God, letting our love and our faith and our understanding be without critical word or phrase, lest we judge who should not judge.

Let our prayer be like these:

You know ——, and what is best for him. Accept my love and gratitude for him, that I may be a channel to him of your blessing and peace.

My heart burns within me that Thy peace and love may rest upon ——. Take my words, my thoughts, my deeds, my all, using them as Thou wilt to bring her Thy love and joy.

26

The Twenty-sixth Week

THE MEDITATION

Thou who art Love, I adore Thee.

My heart burns within. The warmth of Thy presence fills my very being. The glow of wholeness shines about me as I look into Thy Perfection. My breath is quickened, my blood flows with faster beat, my eyes are filled with Thy radiance. I adore Thee, O Thou Eternal One, Joy of my heart and Light of my life.

Thou who art Beauty, I adore Thee.

My ears tingle with the sound of Thy harmonies. The music of the spheres breaks upon my inner being, and I hear Thy voice. Attune my spirit to Thy spirit, O God.

My eyes sparkle with the sight of Thy glory. The color from Thy palette bursts in flame across the heavens, and I behold Thy handiwork in all its majesty. Blessed be Thy loveliness spread before me in field and forest, in flower and tree, in sky and sea.

O God Most Holy, God Most High, I rise before Thee in adoration. Thou art my God, my Love, my Joy, my Life. All that I have I give unto Thee. All that I am I lay before Thee. Accept Thou my sacrifice.

THE PAPER

FELLOWSHIP PROJECTS

Again and again we must check ourselves quite carefully, to make certain that in our search for the will of God we do not turn away from our neighbor. We must realize that we cannot love God and love man without doing more than merely sharing our prayer and meditation. We must try to put our love into action through service every day where possible for someone beyond ourselves. To do this may require the giving of both time and money when we feel we have neither to spare.

Here are hints of the kind of projects that we may enter into as members of the group. We will continue, of course, our present individual action of helpfulness revealing love in action.

1. A book project, giving money for the purchase of devotional books to be sent to new fellowship groups like ours, that they too may have a basic library to help them grow in Christian nurture. This can be done by leaving small or large gifts from time to time in a designated box, or by purchasing books outright and sending them to leaders of new groups.

2. Various pamphlets and reprinted magazine articles of many kinds, informative in the fields of missionary action, social action, personal religious living or Christian education, which may have been a help to you, may be provided for others through the literature table. This is a continuing project which one person might like to handle, seeing that fresh material is kept on the table.

3. Visitation in homes within our parish, where there are shutins who will enjoy our friendship, or folk who may be led through our friendly visit to come into a new understanding of God's presence in their lives. We will not seek to recruit new members for the church or fellowship groups except wholly incidentally; we will try to witness so that these folk too may find what we have found as a beginning to life.

4. Share in friendly visits to nursing homes and the like, taking a program of music or reading or the like, occasionally serving refreshments, and regularly bringing cheer.

5. Call upon new residents within the community, helping to interpret their new location for them. Let them know where the stores, the schools, the churches, the various social events are held. Welcome them to the community even though they are not church folk, and invite them to share in some church of their choice.

6. Invite into your homes foreign students registered in near-by schools, during holiday times, for weekends, or just casually so as to help them see the informality of American home life. If they are interested in the church, invite them to share the service of worship with you.

7. Furnish transportation to various church and community activities to those neighbors who have none, and find the buses inconvenient or inadequate. Search for children who live near you who might be in church school, if someone would transport them. Who knows, that may be the beginning of bringing the parents too!

8. Other projects which we may think of and bring to the fellowship groups. There are many ways of sharing both our time and money, as well as our prayers. Out of our imaginative thinking let us bring such suggestions to the group.

We do not seek another organization to do helpful service. Most of us will continue in the service activities of those organizations to which we now belong. But others of us may need help from one or two or more to meet a need about which we alone are aware. Tell of the need, and others will join you in answering it.

27

The Twenty-seventh Week

THE MEDITATION

Thou hast promised to make my pathway straight, to fill the valleys and to make the high places low. How much easier would be my journey through the days of my life if only this could be! But I have days of steep ascent, when after time of struggle and climbing I suddenly come into the clear vision of the beauty of Thy spirit; only to be followed by days of darkness and gloom when I drop into the bottomless pit of my own despair. If only I did have a pathway upon which to walk where I neither came into the clarity that dazzles nor the confusion that blinds!

Teach me, O God, to see that I am not as yet ready for devotion that is even. I am still worried about myself, without the faith by which I may hold in confidence and trust to Thy love. I would believe—and then I doubt, taking no chances on what may come. I am still fearful for myself, unable to give over my anxiety to Thy love. I would hold to Thy hand—but I want to do what I can to protect myself first. So I drop into the low places, where I do not expect to find Thee. How lonely, how bitter, is the valley of the shadow.

Yet I cannot get away from Thy love. Thou dost long for my return when I hide in the darkness of my own disillusionment. Thou dost call in love to me when I drop into the pit of cynicism. Thou wouldst not that ever I should turn my back upon Thee, for Thou never dost turn Thy face from me.

Grant unto me, Father, clearer sight into Thy love, that the valleys of my despair may be filled and I may come into the high places. Help me to turn from myself, my own gloom, my own discouragement, my own fear, to Thee, that the Light that is in Thee may shine brighter and brighter each day within my heart. Thou art the Eternal One, and I would be patient before Thee. Keep my in my aloneness that I may be alone in Thee.

THE PAPER

ON PATIENCE

Let us learn from nature the rhythm of nature. Jesus told about it in his simple parable: "The earth beareth fruit of herself: first, the blade, then the ear, then the full grain in the ear" (Mark 4:28). There is an orderly process in natural growth. It is to be followed quietly, slowly, carefully.

Act upon the following suggestions as ways to help us find patience and inner quiet in the midst of the confusion and hurry of our normal day.

First, sit down alone in a quiet place and hold your life in your hands. Look at it from all sides. Ask yourself honestly: Why am I hurrying? Why am I impatient? Why are my nerves breaking? Why am I all keyed up?

For one thing, we will find we are moving too fast physically. We hurry to get someplace, hurry to get a job done, just hurry. Patience starts when we begin to slow down. A woman driving

from her suburban home to the city for an appointment found she
was moving too rapidly, hands, feet, mind. She parked her car near
a bus stop, and finished her trip in public transportation. That
forced her to wait, to sit still while another drove according to a
different schedule. Only by that was she able to find patience to
meet her appointment. Move more slowly, so that the body is not
all keyed up, breathless, excited. It will not be easy at first, but
when you catch yourself hurrying, deliberately slow down. We will
think more clearly, more readily when we follow nature's rhythm.

Or again, in our self-examination we will probably find that we
are doing too much. We are good workers, intelligent workers,
unselfish workers who are always accepting the many tasks offered
to us. The work then piles up. Usually it is important work too,
worth while and necessary. If we do not do it, no one will. Yet if we
inwardly are hurried and at odds because of the pressure of our
work, it will be quite worthless. The hardest people to live with are
those so busy doing good that they have no time to *be* good. They
are hurried, irritable, impatient, abrupt. The solution is to stop
doing so much. If we think the world can't get along without us,
perhaps we are correct. But if we are so fussed, so pushing, so
inwardly hurried, our friends will be able to get along without us!

Then too, in examining our life, we will find that some of our
activities are there merely to fill the day. We *must* be *doing* something. We can't sit down alone, for what would we do alone? So,
we join this, that or the other thing, even though we may not care
particularly about them. But we are doing something. The answer
to this is to stop doing and begin being. Be still, be alone, just sit.
Sit and rest, sit and grow patient, sit and think. Catch your breath
physically, don't get into so many things, stop trying to be active,
and sit alone in the quiet. The plant does not hurry itself to grow.
Nor does thought come fast, mental or spiritual thought. The end
of fear, of anxiety, of worry begins when we can sit still and begin
resting creatively.

But that is only half of it. First, we took our life into our hands
to examine it. The beginning of patience is to move more slowly,
to stop trying to save the world in a week, to begin sitting still for
creative rest, thought, study.

Second, comes recognition that underneath all life is the patient God, never hurried, never noisy, but quiet, gentle, slow in action, ever patient. Evelyn Underhill wrote: "God works in tranquillity, and tranquillity seldom goes into partnership with speed." It is through creative waiting, through meditation, through prayer, that we learn the rhythm of God.

Impatiently we say of ourselves: I'm not able to serve God. So Moses spoke, but God in His own time used Moses.

Impatiently we say of ourselves: I'm not fit to serve God until I'm a better man. So Peter spoke, but God took him, and patiently over the years used Peter as He will use us, when we like him are ready to wait.

Impatiently we say of ourselves: We must do it, and do it now. So Judas tried to hurry Jesus and the Kingdom of God, but the Kingdom is still coming in the lives of those who wait, not with resignation, like vegetables stuck in a bin for the winter, but wait in the Lord. For there is our courage. Like the plant, first the blade, then the ear, then the full grain in the ear, we too can grow.

Remember how it is written: Wait on the Lord; be of good courage, and he shall strengthen thine heart; wait, I say, on the Lord.

Examine yourself. Realistically slow down, do less, sit in quiet and meditation, and with faith that God is the author of your courage, learn to live according to nature's rhythm. God moves slowly but surely. When we are willing to do His will, instead of demanding that God do our will, we will begin to know patience.

28

The Twenty-eighth Week

THE MEDITATION

Help me, O God, to live day by day in complete trust in Thy goodness. I remember how blessed the day when I entered into it with faith and trust, how fear disappeared, and anxious moments were forgotten. Even a joyousness came upon me, and I dwelt in the light of Thy spirit. But I do not live that way every day.

I remember in learning to swim how I struggled to make arms and feet move together. I did not dare go beyond my depth, but even in shallow waters I worked furiously. Then I learned slowly to move both arms and legs rhythmically, with careful beat and regular stroke. Now I could go confidently into deep waters.

Yet I went only a little way, lest I become too tired. Once I did hurry to get back to shallow waters, and fear took hold of me. Breathless I returned, but I was afraid for a long time to go out again. Then I learned to float, to rest confidently and buoyantly upon the waters. No longer was I afraid of the deep, for when arms and legs grew tired, I rested upon the softness of the waters.

So teach me to move through the waters of life with equal confidence and trust, stroking easily and regularly with faith and practice, finding that in times of tiredness spiritually I may float restfully upon the vast deep. Renewing my strength, I then would swim on, knowing that "underneath are the everlasting arms."

I do trust in Thy love. I would not be afraid of tomorrow, for it is today in which I live. Myself, my loved ones, my desires I hold before Thee. All that I am or have I place in Thy care. Thou WILT keep him in perfect peace whose mind is stayed on Thee.

THE PAPER

CREATIVE WAITING

Time and again we use this phrase, but what does it mean? It is not putting things off or letting them slide, nor is it "passing the buck" to the Lord. Some folk do these very things to escape from reality.

Creative waiting is putting our lives into God's hands, and listening to His voice, however it may come to us. It may be in the quiet of prayer or of deep thinking late at night or in sudden insight while busy with something else. To hear His voice we must continually hold our life before Him. When all is going well, we thank Him with gratitude and adoration. When we face simple, ordinary problems, we find our resources in Him. Then in time of crisis, when we can turn to no other, because we have always placed ourselves in His hands, we can easily wait with patient trust for His voice. Our complete confidence, our assurance in the love of God, our trust in His wisdom and care, give us strength and courage.

Nels S. Ferré, in his splendid little volume, *Strengthening the Spiritual Life*, suggests that such waiting is living in the perspective, the pace and the proportion of God.

First, living in the perspective of God. Most of us are too involved with the immediate to see any long view. Like Lamentations, we say, "Behold, and see if there be any sorrow like unto my sorrow." We think this both of our personal affairs, so confused are they, and of our national affairs, so tinged with crisis are they. In the perspective of God we see His hand controlling all life, both personal and national. Mature folk knowing history and historical perspective recognize the relationship between today's events and time itself. Mature folk see in the long view how personally an understanding of the pain and struggle of the body can create sympathy, love, helpfulness to others who come into this experience. Joy is of the same. It rests in trust in God's care over all our days, as seen in His perspective. All life is His; hence, there is no fear nor dread at the moment.

Second, accepting the pace of God. God seldom moves fast enough for most of us. We would hurry others into our mold. If we could reform the world, we would do it overnight. Yet God does not work that way. Consider how the Church is the only institution today on a voluntary basis that is a source of power and action for free people. Out of it come both leaders and people ready to be led, though these may not always come directly out of the institution itself. Schuman and Adenauer with their plans for France and West Germany both have come out of Caux and the Moral Rearmament Movement there. Most of the Labour leaders in England in the past generation have come out of the Free Church chapels. God works slowly but surely in bringing forth leaders in society. His pace is the same in our personal life. God freely offers us faith and hope and love, and we are not ready. When we are ready to be used, and have truly accepted commitment as a way of life and not a word of mouth, so that we say to Him: Here am I; fill my days with purpose, Thy purpose; then it is He does use us. God in His own time marvelously accepts us and strangely uses us.

Third, living in the proportion of God. Some folk, though not many, tithe their time, their income, their whole living, giving a proportion regularly to God. The true proportion is giving everything to God, a complete self-abandonment to Him. This means being a Christian lawyer, a Christian carpenter, a Christian housewife, a Christian schoolboy. It is not giving all our money nor even 10 per cent to charity. It means being Christian with all of it, no waste on uncreative, destructive things, but building inner character as well as a fine body. To abandon self to God is the true proportion, the happy one. Then we know we are being used as His agent in raising a family, in handling accounts, in checking deeds, in building homes and churches, in serving through community projects, in deepening one's sense of proportion as a child of God.

Creative waiting is living in the perspective, pace and proportion of God. It is complete and utter assurance in God's care of the inner spirit.

29

The Twenty-ninth Week

The Meditation

This is a sacred place because of the multitudes of hungry folk who have lifted their hearts to Thee in silence, and have been fed. The walls have been beat upon by their prayers, and Thy whisper has quieted their stormings. No denomination, no creed, no sacrament, no dedication itself has made this a holy place. Only the coming together through the years of many like ourselves, seeking forgiveness from Thy mercy, holding a loved one in his need before Thee, asking for Thy wisdom and guidance in making the choices that lie before us, makes this Thy sanctuary. Thou hast been here in times past, and Thy spirit broods upon us in this hour.

Holy, holy, holy, is the Lord God of Hosts! Thy majesty and Thy power overwhelm us. Yet Thy beauty revealed in the glory of the world of nature lifts us out of thralldom to Thee. Thy beauty revealed in the warmth of friendships turns our hearts unto Thee, our Father. Thy children we are, seeking more than awesome wonder before Thy creativity. We would be not servants but friends, friends of God!

Now accept us, Thy children. Accept us with what we have, our weakness and our strength, our ignorance and our knowledge, our sorrow and our joy. Accept us just as we are, human children frail and empty, divine children full of Thy spirit. Accept us where we are, stumbling, halting, yet moving along the Way that is our Truth and Life, even the Way of Jesus the Christ. "And while he was yet afar off, his father saw him, and was moved with compassion, and ran, and fell on his neck, and kissed him."

THE PAPER

THE NEED FOR CONTINUED DISCIPLINE

We are about to come to the end of our first series of thirty weeks together in a fellowship group. During this time we have accepted a simple discipline as the framework of our fellowship together. Now we shall be alone instead of with others, and we must be most careful not to let down. For as soon as we grow lax in our spiritual discipline, we falter. Confusion slips in, our intention is weakened. Sooner or later we find ourselves back where we started from; BUT we don't stop there. Having tasted the fruits of spiritual discipline, we know well what we are missing, so that our condition is worse than before, not better. We can never go back quite to what we were; we will either move ahead patiently and gradually, or we will slip further and further backward. Continued discipline, careful, systematic, meaningful discipline alone will move us forward.

We have agreed to a simple discipline:

1. To pray at least once each day for every other person *by name* in our group.

2. To pray each day for the minister and the congregation for the next Sunday's service of worship.

Some of us have also accepted further discipline, as suggested earlier to the groups. Others of us may wish now to follow this extra fivefold discipline, as suggested by Trueblood in *Alternative to Futility*:

1. To attend at least one service of worship each week.

2. To spend part of each day alone in solitude for private prayer and devotional reading (no agreed length of time, though fifteen minutes has become an accepted period, longer if possible).

3. To get the body and mind still, to listen to the voice of God in silence, with the hope that the minimum of fifteen minutes may become an hour each day.

4. To express each day our love for others through some outgoing activity that is not just for self or the immediate family.

5. To seek simple living in use of time and of money, making both more available to the service both of God and man.

Now has come the period in our growth where we are ready to drop off some of these disciplines or to add on others. Some have found in prayer cells like ours that the following disciplines have proved helpful:

1. To read each day for a period of days or weeks a specific scriptural passage, such as a chapter of Mark each day (same chapter), for a week, trying to find what God would speak through the continued reading; then use another chapter the next week, until the book is completed.

2. To learn by heart the words of some hymn each month, thus enlarging our musical and devotional "vocabulary."

3. To offer grace before each meal.

4. To live frugally, making sure we have enough food, sleep, clothing, but no more than we need, watching our spending carefully, spending of income and time. This discipline may mean a complete rearrangement of one's daily schedule.

5. To tithe regularly, giving a minimum of 10 per cent of one's income to the work of the Lord through the church or charity.

These disciplines are not necessarily for all. For some of us all these are absolutely necessary if we are to grow spiritually. Some of us need to cut down on eating, others to increase, for general health's sake. So with sleeping, with chasing about "doing good," with reading, with visiting, with each phase of our daily life.

Let each one of us face thoughtfully and prayerfully his own condition. Am I lax or am I too strict? Then checking these disciplines and others, let us make for ourselves our own discipline. Let it be in two parts: (1) an agreed discipline for each one of us; (2) a personal discipline for our separate private use.

(For further reading: D. Elton Trueblood's *The Alternative to Futility*, Chapter Four, "The Recovery of Discipline".)

30

The Thirtieth Week

THE MEDITATION

Today is time for appraisal. For weeks we have been experimenting with prayers of many kinds that would bring us into the presence of the living God. All prayer is but a means, not an end. The end is God and His Spirit within us. "Perfect prayer and the love of God are the same thing." This is so, for our prayer, though much of it may be selfish at first, finally becomes a listening to the will of God, in which we become one in His love.

But we hardly would claim to have reached that perfection. We still are striving, humbly knowing that the few steps we have taken, through His mercy and grace, are leading us deeper into fellowship with Him. With St. Paul, "forgetting those things which are behind, and reaching forth unto those things which are before, I press toward the mark for the prize of the high calling of God in Christ Jesus."

What, then, have I found that means bread for my hungry spirit?

Where have I been helped to gain a Center around which my whole life may revolve?

How has God spoken to me in the quiet of my meditation and in the activity of my daily living?

Am I willing to continue the discipline of these few weeks until fellowship with Him is so deep that I no longer need its aid?

Where have I failed to gain answers to questions that lift their heads?

What further resources do I need?

The Paper

DAILY BIBLE READINGS FOR PERSONAL DEVOTIONAL USE

For groups that hold only thirty or so weekly sessions, not meeting during the summer, this lectionary will furnish a balanced reading diet for three months or more. Read these in order, one for each day of the month, then repeat for a second and a third month. Repeated reading will make more familiar these excellent passages. If possible, read them in various translations too.

1. He who is the Happy man, Psalm 1; Matthew 5:3–12
2. God revealed through nature, Psalm 19:1–6; Psalm 150
3. Living day by day, Exodus 16:3–26; Matthew 6:34
4. Heroes of faith, Hebrews 11:1–12:3
5. Fruits of the Spirit, Galatians 5:22–6:10
6. God is our refuge, Psalm 46
7. Steps to growth in character, II Peter 1:5–11
8. How to remember God's blessing, Deuteronomy 6:4–12
9. Law is the word of God, Psalm 19:7–14; Psalm 119:105–112
10. True law is inward, Jeremiah 31:31–34
11. A love idyl, the Book of Ruth (four brief chapters quickly read)
12. Humility is in God's favor, Luke 18:9–14
13. Always in the care of God, Psalm 91
14. A gift of Love, Mark 14:3–9
15. No money needed for the True Bread, Isaiah 55
16. Let no worry fret your day, Luke 12:22–34
17. A creed for Christians, Micah 6:6–8; Luke 10:25–27
18. Sons of light, I Thessalonians 5:1–11
19. A song of judgment that is a new song, Psalm 96

20. When the Spirit of the Lord goes to work, Ezekiel 37:1–14
21. A burden that is light, Matthew 11:25–30
22. Even if God does NOT help, Daniel 3:1–18
23. Bow the knee for this cause only, Ephesians 3:14–20
24. The good shepherd, John 10:1–16
25. A sacrifice overcoming evil, Romans 12
26. Perseverance in prayer, Luke 18:1–8
27. An orderly universe, Genesis 1:1–2:3
28. Be doers as well as hearers, James 1:19–27
29. It is good to go to church! Psalm 84
30. Be not lukewarm, Revelation 3:14–22
31. The best-known Scripture passage, Psalm 23 (to be read slowly)

Suggestions for modern translations of the Bible:

The Complete Bible, An American Translation (Goodspeed and others)

The New Testament, translated by Goodspeed

The Holy Bible, A New Translation (James Moffatt)

The New Testament, translated by Moffatt

New Testament in Modern Speech (Richard Francis Weymouth)

The Old Testament in English (Ronald Knox, Catholic translation)

The New Testament in English (Ronald Knox, Catholic translation)

Holy Bible, Revised Standard Version

The Revised Standard Version of the New Testament

APPENDIX I

Bibliography for Prayer Groups

I. THE NATURE OF PRAYER

Of General Interest

AN AUTOBIOGRAPHY OF PRAYER, Albert E. Day (New York, Harper, 1952).

Out of a moving experience comes this account of the nature, the fruits, the practice of prayer. One of the best introductions to the life of prayer yet to appear.

THE CHOICE IS ALWAYS OURS, ed. by Dorothy Phillips (New York, Richard Smith, 1951).

An anthology of spiritual progression, one of the best to be found, beginning with simple directions and moving into the highest levels of prayer. A large section considers the psychological approach to prayer and meditation. Often the one book found to be the most helpful by thoughtful, alert persons willing to keep growing into spiritual maturity.

THE PERENNIAL PHILOSOPHY, Aldous Huxley (New York, Harper, 1945).

An anthology covering every phase of the spiritual life, with many excerpts from Eastern religions. The worth is greatly enhanced by the vivid commentary of the author—stimulating, thought-provoking, devotional.

PRAYER, George Buttrick (Nashville, Abingdon-Cokesbury, 1942).

An orderly and comprehensive interpretation of prayer in relation to the individual and the world, based on a study of Jesus and his life of prayer. Sound in scholarship and fine in devotional quality, this will be helpful to the reader who lacks a background in the practical aspects of prayer.

PRAYER AND THE COMMON LIFE, Georgia Harkness (Nashville, Abingdon-Cokesbury, 1948).

A nontechnical study of the foundations of prayer, methods of prayer, and the fruits of prayer aimed at creating "vital, God-centered, intelligently grounded prayer." Not a "simple" approach, but written in a popular style.

PRAYER, THE MIGHTIEST FORCE IN THE WORLD, Frank Laubach (New York, Revell, 1946).

A powerful appeal for the practice of intercessory prayer and an interpretation of its effectiveness in terms of modern psychological discoveries.

A PREFACE TO PRAYER, Gerald Heard (New York, Harper, 1944).

An interpretation of prayer for the modern-day intellectual. Based on a wide knowledge of science, psychology and Eastern religions, it is highly stimulating, though difficult.

THE SCHOOL OF PRAYER, Olive Wyon (Philadelphia, Westminster Press, 1944).

Simple to read yet profound in its understanding of the higher stages of prayer, this little book has been helpful to many in interpreting growth in the higher levels.

TEACH US TO PRAY, C. F. Whiston (Boston, Pilgrim Press, 1949).

A study of prayer giving first the theological foundations and then techniques of prayer. There is a fine section on the minister's devotional reading and practice. The bulk of this material has been used frequently in schools of prayer for lay people, where it has been most helpful.

For Advanced Study

CONCERNING PRAYER, B. H. Streeter and Others (New York, Macmillan, 1934).

The nature, difficulties and values of prayer as presented by eleven writers a generation ago. They discuss petition, intercession, worship, prayer and bodily health, the Eucharist and much more. Facing realistically the problems of prayer of their time, these men speak to today's questions as well.

GRACES OF INTERIOR PRAYER, A. Poulain (St. Louis, Herder, 1952).

Highly technical study of interior prayer in all its levels. For the research student or minister who is seeking to understand the many forms of interior prayer.

MYSTICISM, Evelyn Underhill (New York, Dutton, 1945).

A classic in the field of interpretation and description of the life of prayer. The fact that there have been more than a dozen editions of this large book indicates its continuing ability to make the life of prayer understandable and challenging to many people.

PRAYER, Friedrich Heiler (London, Oxford, 1935).

An anthropological study of the history and psychology of prayer in every form, from the primitive man's superstitious petition to the mystic's sublime contemplation. Since it is basic to nearly all modern studies one can scarcely understand the background of the scholarly explorations of prayer without this volume.

ST. JOHN OF THE CROSS, Bede Frost (New York, Harper, 1937).

An introductory study of the Catholic philosophy and practice of interior prayer as found in the writings of the famous Carmelite contemplative. It is a help in understanding this man who is himself necessary reading for those who wish to study the higher levels of prayer.

THE SPIRIT OF LOVE, C. F. Kelly (New York, Harper, 1951).

Based on the teachings of St. Francis of Sales, this excellent interpretation of the renowned spiritual director's philosophy is a "must" for those along the way.

THE THREE AGES OF THE INTERIOR LIFE, Garrigou-Lagrange (St. Louis, Herder, 1948).

No contemporary interpreter of the Catholic understanding of the life of interior prayer is more widely acclaimed than the author of this book. It is a large, two-volume study and is his definitive work on the whole range of the inner life.

II. METHODS OF THE LIFE OF PRAYER FOR BEGINNERS

THE ART OF MENTAL PRAYER, Bede Frost (London, S.P.C.K., 1940).

A statement of the object of mental prayer (better known as meditation) and a description of six classic Catholic methods. Although meditation is one of the beginning practices in prayer this study will appeal more to the persons who take an intellectual approach to the life of the spirit.

CREATIVE PRAYER, E. Herman (New York, Harper, n.d.).

A modern classic, beautifully written, that holds high place as a simple, direct and deep study of the prayer life. It has a fine chapter on silence.

DISCIPLINE AND DISCOVERY, Albert E. Day (Nashville, Upper Room, 1947).

A well-written little book that serves as the manual of discipline for the members of the Disciplined Order of Christ—a spiritual life movement founded by the author—and that has many helpful suggestions for every seeker.

GROWTH IN PRAYER, Constance Garrett (New York, Macmillan, 1950).

A workbook in prayer that tells of the remarkable growth that can come to the person willing to pay the price of careful practice in the devotional life.

HOW RELIGION HELPS, A. W. Palmer (New York, Macmillan, 1949).

A little book of religious helps for convalescents by one who learned through the hard way of overcoming severe illness. Sound in its approach, most helpful from both intellectual and emotional points of view.

INTRODUCTION TO THE DEVOUT LIFE, Francis of Sales (New York, Harper, 1952).

An excellent edition of the French classic, probably the finest guide to spiritual growth for the beginner that has ever been written. It is simple yet deep, full of analogy, humble yet amazingly direct and full of love.

THE LOWER LEVELS OF PRAYER, George Stewart (Nashville Abingdon-Cokesbury, 1952).

For the beginner in prayer this is an excellent study of the first steps in the life. It describes carefully the levels where most folk, both lay and ministerial, practice prayer.

MAKING PRAYER REAL, Lynn Radcliff (Nashville, Abingdon-Cokesbury, 1952).

A sound presentation of the whole range of the life of interior prayer, based on the Catholic masters, but told out of the personal experience and reading of a Protestant minister.

MORE THAN WE ARE, Margueritte Harmon Bro (New York, Harper, 1948).

One of the best introductory guidebooks produced in recent years for beginners. Discusses why, how, posture, place, time and almost every other question facing the beginner in prayer. Especially for women.

ON BEGINNING FROM WITHIN, Douglas Steere (New York, Harper, 1943).

A brief guide to growth in prayer and the devotional life, this book has been used perhaps more than any other as an introduction in cell group study. Its clear interpretation of the prayer life and its suggestions for growth are extraordinarily useful.

PRACTICE OF THE PRESENCE OF GOD, Brother Lawrence (New York, Revell, 1895).

Perhaps the most valuable little guidebook ever written, this brief accounting of some conversations with a saintly monk shows how prayer can be made a living reality in the midst of all the day's activities. Here is the goal of all spiritual striving and one of the most important aspects of the means to it.

PRAYER AND WORSHIP, Douglas Steere (New York, Association Press, 1938).

One of the little books in the Hazen series for college youth, the chapters give a full introduction to private prayer with excellent suggestions for devotional reading in ancient and modern classics.

PRAYER, THE MIGHTIEST FORCE IN THE WORLD, Frank Laubach (See Section I).

PROGRESS THROUGH MENTAL PRAYER, Edward Leen (New York, Sheed and Ward, 1935).

A well-written presentation of the Catholic practice of both the lower and higher levels of prayer, this book gives a clear outline of a system of meditation and many sound suggestions for the practice of the life of prayer.

STRENGTHENING THE SPIRITUAL LIFE, Nels Ferré (New York, Harper, 1951).

A small book that tells inspiringly of the author's experiences of prayer while giving many helpful suggestions for everyone. It is particularly valuable in its discussion of family devotions.

III. METHODS FOR THOSE ALONG THE WAY

THE CLOUD OF UNKNOWING, Anonymous (New York, Harper, 1948).

A classic for its beauty of expression and soundness of teaching. No other book has surpassed this simple book of instruction to those who are passing from acquired to infused prayer.

THE COLLECTED LETTERS OF EVELYN UNDERHILL (New York, Longmans, Green, 1946).

Personal letters of direction and help written to many kinds of people who are searching for spiritual maturity are here brought together for the help of everyone. The collection is a profitable one for both seekers and those who are called upon to give advice about the life of prayer.

HOLY WISDOM, Augustine Baker (New York, Harper, 1949).

One of the most comprehensive and authoritative of all Catholic guidebooks, this large book is a collection of the writings of a famous director. It is much too long and dry for regular reading but is a veritable encyclopedia of sound information.

LETTERS TO A NIECE, Baron Frederick von Hügel (New York, Dutton, 1950).

Although directed entirely to his young niece, these letters by a master of the spiritual life are of great value to others seeking to know answers to the problems of an enlarging devotional life.

LETTERS TO WOMEN, François Fénelon (New York, Longmans, Green, 1909).

A spiritual director of the past gives counsel that is as apt and helpful today as it was three centuries ago.

METHODS OF PRIVATE RELIGIOUS LIVING, Henry N. Wieman (New York, Macmillan, 1929).

Experiments in personal religious living written by a noted philosopher in nontheological language and based on sound psychological techniques.

TRAINING IN THE LIFE OF THE SPIRIT, Gerald Heard (New York, Harper, 1942).

Careful, logical instruction in the life of the spirit that takes the reader into the heights of interior prayer. Brief but effective.

SPIRITUAL EXERCISES, Ignatius Loyola (Westminster, Maryland, New-man, 1943).

The full text of the detailed exercises day by day and week by week as developed by the founder of the Society of Jesus. Much of it can be adapted for Protestant use.

SPIRITUAL LETTERS OF DOM JOHN CHAPMAN (New York, Sheed and Ward, 1944).

These are letters that were for the most part addressed to the problems of full-time "religious" within the Catholic Church and hence are not of general interest. There is much that will be of value to those who are looking for an interpretation of the beginning of contemplative prayer.

WORKS OF ST. JOHN OF THE CROSS (Westminster, Maryland, Newman, 1946). See Section I.

WORKS OF ST. TERESA (New York, Sheed and Ward, 1946).

The experiences and writings of both John of the Cross and his contemporary and friend Teresa of Avila were crucial for the development of the Catholic practice and interpretation of interior prayer. There is much that is relevant to every person's growth in prayer. These books are essential for the earnest student.

IV. DEVOTIONAL

Daily Devotional Reading

THE DAILY ALTAR, Willett and Morrison (New York, Harper, 1919).
An unusually worthy manual, one of the best, used by many Christians during the past forty years.

DEEP IS THE HUNGER, Howard Thurman (New York, Harper, 1951).
Two sections: first, longer meditations used in Thurman's church paper; second, shorter ones, similar in length and mood to those in Part Two of this book, used at the beginning of worship in his Sunday services of worship. Deeply spiritual, keen in devotional insight, warm in sympathy, understanding the social and personal needs of people.

A DIARY OF PRIVATE PRAYER, John Baillie (New York, Scribner, 1949).

Valuable prayers written in the first person to be used morning and evening for thirty-one days. Blank pages are interspersed for the reader's use. Can be read again and again over the months.

EVERY DAY A PRAYER, Margueritte Harmon Bro (New York, Harper, 1943).

Makes a good appeal to the religious beginner who finds nonreligious phraseology more acceptable than the traditional words. The deeply religious experiences that are revealed are moving.

THE MEANING OF FAITH, OF PRAYER, OF SERVICE and THE MANHOOD OF THE MASTER, Harry Emerson Fosdick (New York, Association Press).

Each of the four has daily readings, Scripture, comments and prayer, plus stimulating comment at the end of each week's section. Probably the finest books of their kind for college students. Unsurpassed as study books for prayer cells or for discussion groups, for both men and women.

MEDITATIONS, Toyohiko Kagawa (New York, Harper, 1950).

A hundred and one brief meditations based on scriptural passages, most of them inspiring.

PRAYERS AND MEDITATIONS, Gerald Heard (New York, Harper, 1948).

For the advanced student, prayers and meditations covering thirty-one days, to be repeated month after month. The language is difficult for many but rereading brings understanding. Invaluable for advanced cell groups.

PURITY OF HEART, Søren Kierkegaard, translated by Douglas Steere (New York, Harper, 1938).

A beautiful translation with a discerning introduction by the translator makes this work one of great worth for those who will stay with it. It is designed for the earnest student of prayer.

A SERIOUS CALL TO A DEVOUT AND HOLY LIFE, William Law (London, Everyman, 1951).

A devotional classic from the Protestant tradition in England; a logical straightforward treatise that uses analogies much like the *Pilgrim's Progress*. Its subtle humor makes its teaching stay in the mind.

THE SPIRIT OF ST. FRANCIS OF SALES, Camus, edited and newly translated by C. F. Kelly (New York, Harper, 1952).

Camus was the spiritual son and close friend of Francis and so was in an advantageous position to gather what is one of the most remarkable first-hand accounts of the daily incidents and teachings of a spiritual giant. Here one finds the true spirit of the gentle spiritual director. The book is amazingly effective in helping one to understand the way of Christian love in action.

A TESTAMENT OF DEVOTION, Thomas Kelly (New York, Harper, 1941).

The outstanding devotional classic of modern times, easily understood but revealing spiritual depths not fully grasped except as they are experienced. This series of essays can be reread many times.

THEOLOGIA GERMANICA, Anonymous (New York, Pantheon, 1949).

This edition carries an illuminating introduction to mysticism by Joseph Barnhart and is a clear translation of the fourteenth-century classic favored by Martin Luther. It is one of the basic devotional writings and gives the heart of German mysticism.

Devotional Classics

CHRISTIAN PERFECTION, François Fénelon (New York, Harper, 1947).

Letters of spiritual direction and excerpts dealing with some of the great principles of faith and practice. Beautifully written and profound in insight. Especially suitable for advanced groups.

DOORS INTO LIFE, Douglas Steere (New York, Harper, 1947).

An introduction to five devotional classics: *The Imitation of Christ, Introduction to a Devout Life, John Woolman's Journal, Purity of Heart,* and *Selected Letters of Baron von Hügel.* The author's commentary and interpretation make them live anew.

A GUIDE TO TRUE PEACE, Fénelon, Guyon and Molinos (New York, Harper, 1946).

One of Harper's Golden Series of Devotional Classics. A long-time favorite for those concerned with the Prayer of Quiet. Particularly popular among Quakers.

THE IMITATION OF CHRIST, Thomas a Kempis, Klein edition (New York, Harper, 1947).

The most widely read of all Christian classics. This edition has conveyed the teachings of this ancient work with clarity and in an exceedingly graceful style.

LETTERS OF THE SCATTERED BROTHERHOOD, edited by Mary Strong (New York, Harper, 1948).

Anonymous letters on the spiritual life, some for beginners, many for those moving along the way. Its maturity and spiritual depth challenge to greater devotion.

MEISTER ECKHART, edited by Blakney (New York, Harper, 1941).

An easily read translation of sermons, fragments and legends of a spiritual giant who lived in the fourteenth century.

THE LIFE OF THE SOUL, Samuel Miller (New York, Harper, 1951).

A charmingly written, penetrating and challenging call to everyone to let the life of the soul unfold. It may well become another classic of the spiritual life.

V. BIOGRAPHY

CHARLES FREER ANDREWS, Chaturvedi and Sykes (New York, Harper, 1950).

The story of a devoted Christian missionary who so loved the people of India that he was taken into their lives and homes. He became the close friend and counselor of Gandhi and identified himself with many of the causes for which Gandhi gave himself.

GANDHI'S AUTOBIOGRAPHY (Washington, D. C., Public Affairs Press, 1948).

Many inspiring and revealing biographies of the Indian saint have appeared since his death, but none surpasses in devotional value Gandhi's own account of the first half of his life.

FLAME IN THE SNOW, Iulia de Beausobre (London, Constable, 1946).

A vividly told story of the life of Russia's most loved saint, Serafim of Sarov. Remarkable in its understanding and portrayal of the inner life of a contemplative who returned from his years of isolation to become the spiritual counselor of countless people.

FRANÇOIS DE FÉNELON, Katherine Day Little (New York, Harper, 1951).

The story of the saintly life, work and struggles of one of France's great spiritual directors, whose letters of direction stand high both for their literary worth and their spiritual insight. The book contains a lucid account of the strain of mysticism running through Christianity.

THE JOURNAL OF JOHN WOOLMAN, edited by Janet Whitney (Chicago, Regnery, 1950).

Quakers excel in the art of spiritual autobiographies and this account of the inner and outer life of the saintly Woolman of the eighteenth century is especially outstanding. It rates high as American literature as well as a devotional favorite.

MEN WHO HAVE WALKED WITH GOD, Sheldon Cheney (New York, Knopf, 1948).

The story of many spiritual giants and a weighty presentation of their philosophy and way of life. Considers among others Buddha, Plato, Eckhart, Jacob Boehme and William Blake.

THE LONG LONELINESS, Dorothy Day (New York, Harper, 1952).

The autobiography of the woman who helped Peter Maurin found the *Catholic Worker* and who now carries on as the leader of this courageous group, that lives with the poor in the slums of great cities in the same spirit of love and poverty that characterized Francis of Assisi.

OBERLIN, Marshall Dawson (New York, Willet, Clark, 1934).

This is an account of the Protestant saint of the Swiss mountains whose loving and sacrificial devotion to the poor mountaineers brought their lives to a high level of spiritual and material wellbeing.

PROPHET IN THE WILDERNESS, Herman Hagedorn (New York, Macmillan, 1947.)

This is the biography of Dr. Albert Schweitzer, famous German surgeon, scholar and musician who sacrificed a distinguished career in Europe to found a hospital in the heart of Africa.

ST. FRANCIS OF ASSISI, Paul Sabatier (New York, Scribner, 1909).

One of the best of many biographies of the little brother who is proclaimed by many as the Christian who has most truly imitated the life of Christ.

TOYOHIKO KAGAWA, THE CHRISTIAN, J. K. Van Baalen (Grand Rapids, Eerdman's, 1936).

This is a narrative of Japan's most famous and inspirational Christian leader, the man who began his Christian life by sharing his tiny room with beggars and harlots in the slums of Shinkawa and who went on to become one of Japan's most significant social reformers and religious spokesmen.

VI. PRAYER GROUPS

Books

FELLOWSHIPS OF CONCERN, Harvey Seifert (Nashville, Abingdon-Cokesbury, 1949).

A full-length treatment of the need and practice of cells, particularly those common on college campuses.

ALTERNATIVE TO FUTILITY, D. Elton Trueblood (New York, Harper, 1948).

The chapter on the Fellowship of the Concerned deals with the need and nature of cells. It is especially valuable for its concrete suggestions for personal and group disciplines in the search for growth in prayer.

THE SECRET OF LIFE, Roy A. Burkhart (New York, Harper, 1950).

Suggestions for prayer groups as developed in First Community Church, Columbus, Ohio. This book presents the philosophy of the full-guidance church rather than suggesting techniques for cell group activity.

TOWARD FELLOWSHIP WITH GOD AND MAN, Harold Chance (Philadelphia, A.F.S.C., 1948).

The last chapter discusses the cell as a specific means for achieving the fellowship indicated in the title.

SAY YES TO THE LIGHT, Allan Hunter (New York, Harper, 1946).

A man who has been the influential founder and leader of innumerable cells tells in this book of the part they can play in spiritual growth.

Pamphlets

CELLS FOR PEACE, Douglas Steere (New York, Fellowship Press).

The nature and methods of a workout cell that has world peace as its dominant concern.

CREATING CHRISTIAN CELLS (New York, Evangel).

Many accounts of the fruits of prayer groups at work.

FELLOWSHIP CELLS FOR CHRISTIAN LIVING, Ruth Seabury (Boston, Pilgrim Press).

Primarily intended for campus use in the founding and carrying on of intimate groups devoted to the spiritual search.

GROUP DISCUSSION IN RELIGIOUS EDUCATION, Harrison S. Elliott (New York, Y.M.C.A., 1930).

An invaluable aid to the cell leader whose responsibility it is to conduct the seeking and sharing and study of his group along creative lines.

PRAYER GROUPS (New York, Board of Missions of the Methodist Church).

Practices of cell groups and examples of their operation.

PRAYER GROUPS, Norman K. Elliott (United Prayer Tower, 1951).

Techniques for groups mainly concerned with intercession.

PRAYER GROUPS AND HOW TO CONDUCT THEM, Helen Shoemaker (New York, Calvary House).

Similar to the above.

SPIRITUAL POWER THROUGH FELLOWSHIP CELLS (Chicago, United Christian Youth Movement, 1944).

Material similar to that in Seifert's book.

THOUGHTS ON THE FORMATION OF A PRAYER GROUP (Spiritual Life Clinic).

Similar to the two pamphlets called *Prayer Groups*.

TOWARDS THE CONVERSION OF ENGLAND, A Commission (Westminster, Church Assembly, 1945).

A plan of evangelism for the Anglican Church prepared by an official committee that tells of the part that small groups can have in the larger work of the church.

Leaflets

HOW TO START A CELL; HOW TO KINDLE THE GROUP; TOWARDS INCREASING EFFECTIVENESS, all by Irving Harris (New York, The Evangel).

Stimulating, succinct suggestions for the operation of sharing cells.

PRAYER CELLS AND EVANGELISM, Samuel Shoemaker (New York, National Council of the Churches of Christ).

A persuasive presentation of the prayer cell as a means of bringing a new Pentecost.

Periodical

LIFE-STREAM (Berkeley, California).

A periodical leaflet telling of cell experiences and giving suggestions for their procedure. World-wide concern.

VII. RETREATS

THE CONDUCTING OF RETREATS, James Wareham (London, Mowbray, 1950).

The nature of retreats and the methods of conducting them as seen from the point of view of Anglicanism. Concerned with the silent, directed retreat.

RETREATS AND HOW TO CONDUCT THEM, Symposium (London, A.P.R., 1947).

Similar to the above.

RETREATS FOR PROTESTANTS, John Oliver Nelson (Bangor, Pennsylvania, Kirkridge).

A pamphlet that interprets the idea of retreats from the point of view of the free churches, utilizing elements of the traditional forms of retreats but providing for sharing and guidance among all involved, the form developed successfully at Kirkridge.

TIME TO SPARE, Douglas Steere (New York, Harper, 1947).

The only full-length book in America discussing retreats from the point of view of Protestants, although it holds closer to the traditional form than does the Kirkridge pamphlet. It gives almost every detail necessary for the setting up of a three-day retreat and then provides devotional materials that may be used in such a retreat, including material that may be read at mealtimes. This latter material may well be used by an individual for his own devotional life.

APPENDIX II

Addresses of Movements Concerned with Prayer Groups

CALVARY HOUSE, 61 Gramercy, New York 10, New York. Publishers of *The Evangel* and many reprints from it concerning cell groups; sponsors of a number of cells; source of information and counsel on groups.

CAMPS FARTHEST OUT, 1571 Grand Avenue, St. Paul 5, Minnesota. Many prayer groups concerned particularly with intercession for peace and for health have come into being out of the work of this spiritual movement.

DISCIPLINED ORDER OF CHRIST, Mt. Vernon Place Methodist Church, Baltimore, Maryland. Source of information and counsel on cell groups.

FELLOWSHIP OF RECONCILIATION, 21 Audubon Avenue, New York 32, New York. Publishers of *Cells for Peace* and source of information and counsel for cells of this kind, of which it sponsors many.

INTERNATIONAL CHRISTIAN LEADERSHIP, 2324 Massachusetts Avenue, N.W., Washington, D.C. A businessmen's organization that cultivates world-wide interest in cells devoted to prayer and peace.

KINGWOOD COMMUNITY, Frenchtown, New Jersey. A full Christian community that came into being through the extension of a cell experience; a source of information and counsel on groups.

KIRKRIDGE FELLOWSHIP, R.F.D., Bangor, Pennsylvania. A Christian fellowship under a discipline, a retreat and study center in the mountains and a sponsor of cells. Holds periodical training and retreat conferences for cell groups leaders.

THE LAYMEN'S MOVEMENT FOR A CHRISTIAN WORLD, 347 Madison Avenue, Room 1402, New York 17, New York. The founder of the meditation room at the United Nations, sponsors of training groups for cell leadership at Wainwright House, Rye, New York, a source of information and counsel on prayer groups.